Effective Coaching
Second Edition

To learn more about titles in the Briefcase Books series go to
www.briefcasebooks.com

Effective Coaching
Second Edition

Marshall J. Cook and Laura Poole

McGraw-Hill

New York Chicago San Francisco Lisbon
London Madrid Mexico City Milan New Delhi
San Juan Seoul Singapore Sydney Toronto

10 11 12 13 14 15 LCR 21 20 19 18 17

ISBN	978-0-07-177111-5
MHID	0-07-177111-5
e-ISBN	978-0-07-177253-2
e-MHID	0-07-177253-7

This is a CWL Publishing Enterprises book developed for McGraw-Hill by CWL Publishing Enterprises, Inc., Madison, Wisconsin, www.cwlpub.com.

Library of Congress Cataloging-in-Publication Data

Cook, Marshall
    Manager's guide to effective coaching / by Marshall Cook and Laura Poole — 2nd ed.
    p. cm.
    ISBN-13: 978-0-07-177111-5 (pbk. : acid-free paper)
    ISBN-10: 0-07-177111-5 (pbk. : acid-free paper)
    1. Employees—Coaching of. 2. Employees—Training of. 3. Employee motivation. 4. Mentoring in business. 5. Supervision of employees. I. Poole, Laura. II. Title.

HF5549.5.C8C666 2011
658.3'124—dc23

                                                                    2011019484

McGraw-Hill books are available at special quantity discounts to use as premiums and sales promotions, or for use in corporate training programs. To contact a representative, please e-mail us at bulksales@mcgraw-hill.com.

This book is printed on acid-free paper.

Contents

Preface

I f you've ever played on a sports team, you've had a coach. A good sports coach gives the team the tools to succeed, guides them, helps them do their best, and cheers them on as they perform. Coaches help you learn from failures, celebrate your successes, and find and use all the resources within you.

In the business world, coaching has caught fire as a method to empower, engage, and develop employees and top talent. Many top executives use coaches and credit the coaching relationship for their success levels. Two studies in 2001 indicated that the return on investment of executive coaching was five to seven times the initial cost, measured through improvements in productivity, quality, communication, relationships, and other areas. Coaching also significantly improves intangible benefits (employee retention, teamwork, job satisfaction). A survey of Fortune 500 companies found that up to 40 percent used executive coaching services. Another survey found that 86 percent of all companies use executive coaches. Clearly, coaching is a powerful and useful technique for growth, and today's business world recognizes that fact.

In this book, you'll learn how to apply good coaching methods in the workplace, helping employees achieve high performance by seeking commitment rather than control and results rather than somebody to blame.

As we describe the main functions of the coach in the workplace and examine the structure of an effective coaching session, we stress coaching on the run, where you'll really do your best work. Two simple principles guide us: KYHO (keep your hands off) and PSA (positive specific action).

We discuss the skills, techniques, and pitfalls to good coaching and help you understand the best ways to avoid them. We cover how to bring a coach approach to your other responsibilities as manager, such as that of trainer, mentor, and corrector. We offer specific tools and techniques you can use right away.

By studying worker motivations beyond the paycheck, you'll learn to challenge employees to achieve and learn. You'll also learn to communicate and listen effectively, by giving clear instructions and by asking effective questions and hearing the answers.

You'll learn to use intrinsic, intangible rewards—ownership, mastery, and growth—to spur peak performance while fostering independence and initiative.

The bonus principles described in Chapter 15 will help your coaching and all other aspects of your life—because coaching will become a vital part of your life and give you skills to apply outside the workplace as well.

Are you ready? Let's get going.

Special Features

The idea behind the books in the Briefcase series is to give you practical information written in a friendly person-to-person style. The chapters deal with tactical issues and include lots of examples. They also feature numerous sidebars designed to give you different types of specific information. Here's an overview of the types of sidebars and what they cover.

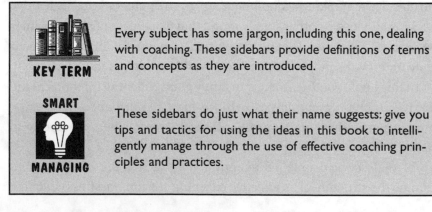

KEY TERM
Every subject has some jargon, including this one, dealing with coaching. These sidebars provide definitions of terms and concepts as they are introduced.

SMART MANAGING
These sidebars do just what their name suggests: give you tips and tactics for using the ideas in this book to intelligently manage through the use of effective coaching principles and practices.

Tricks of the Trade sidebars give you insider how-to hints on techniques astute managers use to execute the tactics described in this book.

It's always useful to have examples that show how the principles in the book are applied. These sidebars provide descriptions of on-the-job situations where effective coaching improves performance and relationships.

Caution sidebars provide warnings for where things could go wrong when implementing coaching practices and things you should be aware of to help prevent problems.

How can you make sure you won't make a mistake when you're trying to implement the techniques the book describes? You can't, but these sidebars give you practical advice on how to minimize the possibility of things going wrong.

This icon identifies sidebars where you'll find specific procedures, techniques, or technology you can use to successfully implement the book's principles and practices.

Acknowledgments

The authors thank John Woods of CWL Publishing Enterprises, who worked to develop the original manuscript and then committed to this thorough update.

About the Authors

Marshall J. Cook is professor emeritus, Division of Continuing Studies at the University of Wisconsin–Madison. He is the author of more than 30 books, including *Slow Down and Get More Done*, *Time Management*, and the first edition of *Effective Coaching*. He edits Extra Innings, an online newsletter for writers and for 20 years has edited a print publication for writers called *Creativity Connection*. He has published articles and short stories in hundreds of regional and national magazines, and is a columnist for The Perspiring Writer, an online magazine for writers. He teaches in the Odyssey Project for the University of Wisconsin–Madison. Marshall holds a BA in creative writing and an MA in communications from Stanford University.

Laura Poole is an Associate Certified Coach (ACC), credentialed by the International Coach Federation. She is the founder of her own coaching practice, Archer Coaching, and specializes in helping working professionals create a meaningful career balanced with a joyful life. She works with teams, companies, and individuals to create lasting change, powerful results, and new ways of thinking and doing. She is also an avid public speaker on a variety of topics.

After graduating from Duke University, Laura began her career in publishing. She eventually founded her own freelance editorial services company in 1997, through which she provides scholarly copy editing for major publishers. She also co-developed a respected editing training program for freelancers and publishers. Her shift into the coaching field came in 2007 when she decided to seek work that had a meaningful impact on the world. Visit her Web site at www.archercoaching.com.

Laura lives in Durham, North Carolina, with her family. You can reach her at laura@archercoaching.com.

The Goals of Good Coaching

Morale in the desktop publishing group is low. Some of the employees seem to work furiously every day, but Molly seems to have time to kill. No deadlines have been missed, but the hard-working group seems resentful of the slacker, and she distracts others when she wanders around the office chatting or sits at her computer playing solitaire. You have been getting complaints about Molly, and it's your responsibility to address this issue. What's your first move?

We'll return to this situation after you learn about the goals of good coaching and how management with coaching will help you get the information you need to work toward a solution.

Why Should a Manager Be a Coach?

Coaching is a relatively new field of development (see Chapter 2 for definitions and distinctions of what coaching is). It's quickly growing in popularity, both as a stand-alone profession and as a tool set for business leaders. Coaching in the workplace can create a positive environment in which employees are empowered, engaged, and valued. In teams, coaching can foster better communication, synergistic thinking, and productivity. For individuals, good coaching can lead to career development, increased resourcefulness, personal empowerment, sustainable change and improvement, and bigger thinking.

Managers and supervisors are often expected to be role models, mentors, leaders, and now coaches. Adding coaching to your skill set not only improves your value in the workplace, it creates new opportunities for your employees and the organization as a whole.

Are You Tapping Your Most Valuable Resource?

Employees offer an enormous source of only partially tapped potential. Each person in a workplace has a specific job, but people are rarely limited to a narrow category. There is much that each employee can offer, in terms of his or her own job performance, creative ideas, skills, and strengths to put to use for the organization, and personal growth and learning. Are you tapping this valuable resource? Connecting with your employees through coaching can open up far more possibilities than you might imagine!

Research by Gallup (Harter, Schmidt, Killham, and Agrawal, Q^{12} Meta-Analysis, August 2009) studying the link between employee *engagement* and performance indicated that highly engaged business/work teams basically doubled their odds of success! Employee engagement is a strategic foundation, not just lip service from human resources. Gallup has shown that engaged workers are more productive, profitable, loyal, and customer focused. In addition, their research discovered that consistently, an employee's immediate manager had the most profound impact on his or her retention and satisfaction.

GALLUP

TOOLS

To learn more about Gallup's extensive research into employee engagement and great managers, see www.gallup.com/consulting/52/ employee-engagement.aspx. The best-selling book *First, Break All the Rules* (Marcus Buckingham and Curt Coffman; Simon & Schuster, 1999) discusses Gallup's research in depth and describes the Q^{12}, the 12 questions used to assess employee engagement.

Accessibility

Your Accessibility quotient is your openness to input from your staff. (It also gives some insight into how engaged employees are.) How would your workers respond to the following statements? Answer "yes" or "no" as you think they would *really* respond, not as you'd like them to.

My boss:

1. asks for my opinion frequently.
2. listens to my suggestions.
3. takes my ideas seriously.
4. values my opinion.
5. checks with me before making a decision that affects my work.
6. would defend me in a meeting of supervisors.
7. explains goals clearly when giving me a new project.
8. welcomes my questions about an ongoing project.
9. gives me latitude in deciding how to carry out a project.
10. saves criticism for one-on-one sessions.

Engagement Being fully involved in, enthusiastic, and committed to the work, goals, and mission of an organization. **KEY TERM**

MORE VIEWPOINTS
To get a reality check on your accessibility as measured by your employees, ask them the ten questions through an anonymous survey or as part of a 360 evaluation of your role. **TOOLS**

Your Responses and Your Management Style

Did you rack up seven or more positive responses in the Accessibility quiz? If so, you already exhibit many of the attributes of a good coach. One of the main goals of management by coaching is to create an atmosphere in which employees are willing and able to share their ideas with a superior. When employees feel heard and valued, they are more invested in their work and the organization.

Getting fewer than seven positive responses doesn't mean you're a failure. A low score means you have some work to do. (A lower score may also indicate that you're more honest and self-critical than most managers.)

Let's look at each statement and what it indicates about your working relationship with your employees.

1. My boss asks for my opinion frequently. The people who work with you already know you don't have all the answers. When you ask for an employee's input, three good things happen, before you even get a

WATCH OUT FOR ATTITUDE

CAUTION If you hesitated before answering some of these questions, you may be revealing a lack of awareness of workers' attitudes. If so, pay particular attention to tips in this book on becoming sensitive to employee feedback, which includes written and oral messages, body language, and other indicators.

response: (1) you show respect for the employee, (2) you show that you don't think you have a corner on wisdom, and (3) you open yourself to an opportunity to get valuable information. "How do you think we should handle it?" can be one of the best things you ever ask an employee.

2. My boss listens to my suggestions. Asking is only half the process. Listening is the other half (see Chapter 6 for more on listening skills). Give employees your full attention. Indicate by word and gesture that you're taking in what they say. Ask questions. Respond honestly.

3. My boss takes my ideas seriously. You say, "Uh huh. That's ... interesting." The employee hears, "Thanks for nothing. Now we'll do it my way." You won't necessarily agree with employees' perspectives, and you may not act on their suggestions. But if they offer the input sincerely, you should take it seriously. If you think an idea has merit, say so. If you think

WALK THE WALK

CAUTION Unfortunately, many employees go to work every day without ever being asked for their opinions. They won't expect you to want that input unless you ask for it, and they may not trust you when you do. Be patient, back up your words with actions, and you'll eventually earn their trust and candor.

it's flawed, explain why. Discuss ideas, not personalities. Don't allow the discussion to become a battle between "your idea" and "their idea" or a contest with a winner and a loser.

4. My boss values my opinion. You show that you value an opinion by listening to it, tak-

ing it seriously, and rewarding it. Most businesses reward results—jobs successfully completed, goals reached, bottom lines enriched—if they reward employee performance at all. Appreciation should begin much earlier in the process, when you're looking for hard work, cooperation, and creative input.

It takes courage and initiative for an employee to speak up. Reward that courage through your words and deeds. Questions and suggested alternatives are positive contributions, not threats.

5. My boss checks with me before making a decision that affects my work. You're the boss, and you make the decisions. When a decision affects working conditions, you should talk it over with employees and get their input first—not only to show that you respect them, but also to help you make the best decision.

6. My boss would defend me in a meeting of supervisors. Are you willing to go to bat for your employees, fight for them, defend them from unjust attacks, and take your share of the blame when something goes wrong?

Would your workers say that you're a "stand-up boss"? There's no higher praise they can give you.

7. My boss explains goals clearly when giving me a new project. Employees are no better at reading your mind than you are at reading theirs. When you assign a task, do you take the time to outline in clear, simple terms exactly what should be accomplished? An employee who understands the overall purpose of her work will do a better job and feel better about doing it. And you'll prevent costly mistakes down the line.

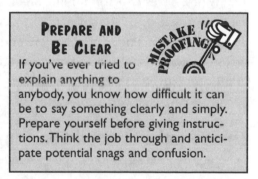

PREPARE AND BE CLEAR

If you've ever tried to explain anything to anybody, you know how difficult it can be to say something clearly and simply. Prepare yourself before giving instructions. Think the job through and anticipate potential snags and confusion.

8. My boss welcomes my questions about an ongoing project. "Do you understand?" When most folks ask that question, they expect a quick "yes" (the same way most of us expect a perfunctory "Fine, thanks" when we ask, "How are you?").

Employees' questions will seem like interruptions and irritations—unless you train yourself to expect and welcome them. Questions are often the only way you really know what an employee has heard and understood. Employees willing to ask you a question now—knowing that they won't be penalized for showing "ignorance"—will do a better job.

> ### GIVING INSTRUCTIONS
>
> **FOR EXAMPLE** Be careful about the amount and nature of the directions you give. Make sure that directions are appropriate to the situation. "I want you to increase sales by 5 percent in the next quarter" may be enough of a charge for a trusted salesperson with experience, product knowledge, and the necessary authority to do the job (for example, the ability to negotiate the terms of an offer or to spend up to a set amount for increased promotion). However, "I want you to make 30 copies of each of these handouts, and I want you to do it by taking them down to the copy machine and setting the counter to 30 and feeding in the originals one at a time" is probably a whole lot more instruction than most people need—or appreciate.

9. My boss gives me latitude in deciding how to carry out a project. Explain goals clearly and precisely. Answer all questions. But don't always spell out exactly how those goals should be reached. Whenever possible, leave room for creativity and initiative.

10. My boss saves criticism for one-on-one sessions. Praise in public, criticize in private—not so that people will think you're a nice person but because it works. Public criticism engenders defensiveness and anger— in the employee criticized and in everybody else within earshot. Criticism in private, delivered decisively but respectfully, has a much better chance of getting you what you want—improved performance.

The Benefits of Good Coaching

Effective coaching moves an employee from WIIFM (what's in it for me?) to WIIFU (what's in it for us?)—essentially, creating a higher level of engagement. It enables you, as the coach, to reap specific benefits from your efforts. Let's look at the advantages you can derive from being a successful coach.

Develop Employees' Competence

Watch a loving parent initiate a child into the mysteries of riding a bicycle. First the parent instructs the child and then shows how it is done. But at some point the kid has to climb on that bicycle and ride it alone.

Now imagine that you're the loving parent, running beside the wobbling bike, shouting encouragement, your hand first tightly clutching the handle bars and then gradually loosening your grip until finally, your heart in your throat, you let go, launching your child into the world.

Now imagine that you're the child on the bike. You're terrified and exhilarated, concentrating on keeping the

SUCCESS BUILDS ON ITSELF SMART
The goal of good coaching isn't just to help employees reach a certain performance level. It's important to realize that one MANAGING success engenders another and instills the self-confidence that leads to higher levels of motivation and performance in many areas.

pedals pumping and the bike from falling over. But at some point—hours, days, or maybe even weeks later—you realize that the balancing act, at first seemingly impossible, has become second nature. You don't have to think about riding the bike; you can just do it—and enjoy it.

Coaching is similar. A good coach helps workers "learn to fly" without regular coaching. And that's the point. Good coaches create situations where they're no longer needed.

Diagnose the Roots of Performance Problems

If employees aren't performing at peak efficiency, you have to figure out the reasons behind it. Too often, getting input from the people closest to the job, the employees themselves, is overlooked.

A good coach asks for employee input and then listens carefully to it. By doing so, you're more likely to make an accurate assessment, discover the deepest roots of the issue, and get cooperation and investment in arriving at a solution. If employees feel empowered to solve the problem, they'll solve it.

KEEP AN OPEN MIND SMART
When you seek root causes for problems, be ready to abandon assumptions. You may assume, for example, that the MANAGING person closest to the origin of the problem is responsible for it. But if you keep an open mind, you might find the bottleneck elsewhere, perhaps even at the supervisory level.

Change Unsatisfactory or Unacceptable Performance

Once you have found the source of a problem or unacceptable performance, you can decide how to go about creating a change. Here again,

SMART

MANAGING

DEAL WITH THE PROBLEM
"Don't shoot all the dogs just because one of them's got rabies," Paul Newman as Hud Bannon (in *Hud*) advises.

If you determine that a problem lies with one person's phone-answering performance, don't send all the employees to a training session on phone etiquette. Work (or arrange to have someone else work) with the specific employee on the specific issue. In this way, you won't waste anybody else's time, and you won't create resentment.

don't overlook a rich potential source of solutions—the employees themselves. Brainstorm with a group of employees and let them help you evaluate potential actions. When workers are asked about their thoughts and potential solutions, they become more invested in the process. They might get more excited about making a change, and they will feel valued because they were heard. Creating a change *with* a group, instead of handing down a decision without input, gets buy-in from the start.

Address a Behavioral Issue

Behavioral problems are sticky territory in the workplace. Performance is at least somewhat objective. You can count outputs and actions taken, and you can compare today's performance with yesterday's and mine with yours. But evaluating employees' behavior is often a matter of assessing attitude and demeanor.

You may think that some employees spend too much time chatting about personal matters when they should be tending to business. But how much time is "too much"? Others may view your workplace and comment on the friendliness and apparent cooperation among staff members. You're on safer ground when you confine employee evaluations to measurable outputs. If chatty employees are getting their work done, that work is satisfactory, and their conversation isn't bothering anyone else, the "problem" may be nothing more than your own irritation.

Behavioral guidelines are often vague, but the stakes can be staggeringly high—in lawsuits and grievances alleging discrimination, for example.

Using the basic principles of good coaching is important in these situations. Involve relevant employees in defining the situation and in determining whether behaviors are getting in the way of performance.

Check to make sure the "problem" isn't irritation on your part. Keep an open mind, and keep your assumptions to yourself. Be willing to explain any decisions you may make to address the issues, along with options for appeal to a higher level.

For example, imagine that three of the four members of

MAKE THEM AWARE **SMART**

It's not unusual for employees to complain that coworkers are bothering them. When this happens, those doing the **MANAGING** bothering are frequently unaware of how their behavior affects others. Often the situation can be improved by sensitively informing the offending individuals how others feel and by seeking suggestions on how to make improvements.

your office staff are chatting happily; the fourth is seething. Patti finds this distracting and annoying, she tells you, especially when she's on the phone with a potential client. She feels that her own job performance is suffering. She also lets you know, without saying so directly, that she doesn't see how the others could possibly be getting their work done with all that conversation. She wants permission to listen to her MP3 player so that she can use music to screen out the noise.

There's more than one way forward here: huddle up with *all* the players and talk it through. You'll learn how to conduct these sessions, step by step, in later chapters. You'll get the results you want—and you'll save time. Plus, you'll have group buy-in, awareness, and investment in change.

Foster Productive Working Relationships

"Works well with others." When we were growing up, teachers let parents know on report cards how we were getting along with the other kids. We went to school to learn social skills (take turns, share the crayons, no kicking, and so on) as well as academic subjects.

In an office setting, people are not graded on their social skills—at least not in so many words. Companies set performance objectives but still talk about intangibles like "attitude" and whether an employee is a "team player." They still want people to work well with others; they just call it something else.

As you apply the techniques of coaching in the workplace, you'll notice better performance from your employees and also employees helping each other. When you set the example, people take the hint and start coaching each other to higher levels of performance. You can't order them to do it, but it can happen without your saying a thing.

Create Opportunities for Conveying Appreciation

Many of us have a hard time saying "Thank you" or "Good job." We lack formal occasions and established patterns for giving praise, and we find it difficult to ad lib.

Coaching provides natural opportunities to praise good work and strong effort.

Foster Self-Coaching Behaviors

As you become an effective coach, you'll find that employees will become more competent. When you coach an employee through a challenge, you teach him or her to figure out how to deal with similar problems in the future and tap inner personal resources.

Remember: Your role goes beyond getting specific tasks completed. It's about creating more competent and committed employees who have the ability to add ever-higher levels of value to the organization.

Improve Employee Performance, Engagement, and Morale

Call it morale, self-esteem, or whatever you want. How your staff members feel about themselves and their roles in the workplace makes a big difference in their performances.

Coaching employees with respect does a lot to improve morale and engagement. It also affects their performance. By allowing employees to take responsibility and initiative for their work, you'll empower them, and thus improve their morale in ways no seminar, pep talk, or self-help book ever could.

This final point, then, is the culmination of all those already listed. As you increase performance through coaching, you also improve morale and engagement. Your ability to coach effectively communicates to employees that you care about them and are committed to helping them improve. This can translate into commitment and excitement about their work. And this naturally leads to higher performance and higher morale. In other words, all these actions go together, and coaching is the method that makes it happen.

Meanwhile, Back at the Publishing Group

Let's go back to the story at the beginning of this chapter. Along with complaints from the other desktop publishers, you hear from the writers and project managers that Molly distracts them when she constantly "pops in" to their offices to say hello. You've noticed that she seems distracted, bored, and disengaged. What are your options?

1. Send the entire publishing department to a team-building event. Maybe that will improve morale and get Molly back to work.
2. Warn Molly about the problem, give her three months to shape up, and put a note in her personnel file. She needs to shape up or get out.
3. Send Molly to a training workshop on the software she uses. She's probably trying to do a good job, maybe she just doesn't know how to use the software correctly.
4. Rearrange the work flow system. You may be able to fix the problem without upsetting anyone.
5. Do nothing. The situation might work itself out when things simmer down. Besides, Molly has made no secret about being unhappy with her job. Maybe she'll leave soon.

What's your call, coach?

None of the above. At this stage, you don't know enough about the problem to create a solution. You need more information—and one of the best sources for it is sitting in her cubicle right now, playing another game of solitaire because she's so bored.

In later chapters, we discuss the best ways to get that information. For now, let's imagine a conversation that will give you a good sense of how a skillful coach might handle the situation.

You: I'd like to take a look at the way we handle work flow. Can you give me a few minutes to explain the system to me?

Molly: Sure. (She explains how the desktop publishers work in teams with the writers and project managers, so that one person might be deluged with new projects all at once, whereas another might only have clean-up work, revisions, or be waiting for new assignments.)

You: So in that case, the whole team has to wait for their specific publisher to get around to their project?

Molly: Yep. They try to schedule the projects so they don't end up down here all at once, but we all know how well *that* works [rolls her eyes]. Nothing really stays on schedule; it usually runs long or sometimes short, so the schedules are more like wishful thinking.

AVOID SARCASM

In a conversation like this, there may be a tendency for an employee to get sarcastic. It's important not to respond negatively to this. You should also not become sarcastic in response, or neither of you will take the conversation seriously and your mutual respect may be undermined. Instead, ignore the sarcasm and keep the conversation focused on information gathering and problem solving.

You: It sounds like a single publisher can get really overloaded and another might not have much to do.

Molly: You got that right. I know everyone is really busy these past few months, but I haven't had as much to do, and I know they resent me for it. I see them glaring at me, and sometimes I hear them talking behind my back.

You: Do you have any ideas as to why you haven't seemed as busy as the others?

Molly: Oh, several. For one thing, I work pretty fast, so I can finish my work on a particular book a little faster than someone else might. I'm only on two teams right now, and most of the others are on at least three. Both of my teams seem to be at "in-between" stages, waiting on some graphics or material before coming to me, so I'm in a holding pattern. I *was* on a third team, but with that round of layoffs a few months ago, that team was let go and their work reassigned.

You: Do the others ever ask you to help them out if they are behind?

Molly: Sometimes. I'm happy to help them. But when the team structure was rolled out, the brass seemed interested in keeping things consistent with just one publisher on each project, without spreading the workload out, so we've all been leery of asking for help.

You: I get the sense that you don't *want* to be bored.

Molly: Oh heck no! I would rather be busy than bored. It's frustrating.

You: Well, what could you do if you don't have any assigned work on your schedule?

Molly: I'm not sure. With the team structure as it is, I don't think the others will let me help with their projects. We tend to get territorial about them.

You: OK, if you're not helping on a specific project, what else might you do?

Molly: Hmm. I've noticed that we don't seem to have a set procedure for how raw documents are typeset and how revisions are handled. I've made up some of my own checklists and flow charts, because I like having them. Tim saw them and wanted to use them, too, so he has copies. Maybe I could use those to create some forms for the whole department.

You: Wow, that sounds really helpful! I'd like to see them, too.

Molly: Okay, I can start that today.

You: Great! What else could you do?

Molly: Well, I've noticed that sometimes the writers get bogged down in checking the revisions, which can really delay a project. I used to do some proofreading at my last job, and I could do that here. Maybe I could do a quick review of a revision, flag any errors that need to be fixed, and then either send it back to the writers or give it back to the publishers to fix.

You: That sounds like it might be helpful. Would that work in the team structure?

Molly: I think so, because it would be a new role, instead of taking over for someone already doing it. Plus, having a fresh set of eyes on a piece can be helpful. If you've seen a particular piece a number of times, it gets harder to spot the errors. I learned that working for a magazine.

You: I think I can support you there. Let's try it out with one team for a week or two, and if it works well, then I'll alert the other writers to do the same.

Molly: Sounds good.

You: Thanks for your insights, Molly. Let me know how your procedural forms go, and how the proofreading works out.

Molly: Will do!

That's how the dialog *might* go. However it proceeds, you can expect the interchange to be productive when employees trust you enough to express themselves freely with the expectation that you're there to help. It's likely that you'll make progress toward a solution even if you don't solve the problem outright.

That's what this book is all about—helping you achieve peak employee performance and engagement through good coaching. Read on.

The Coach's Checklist for Chapter 1

☑ If you're not developing your people, you're wasting your most valuable resource.

☑ How accessible are you, and how engaged are your employees? If you didn't take the accessibility quiz, go back and do it now.

☑ Coaching is good for employees, and it's good for managers as well. Coaching builds relationships that result in continuously improved performance for you and your employees.

The Attributes of a Good Coach

Clarke Stallworth glowered at the room full of skeptical editors.

"I used to be really tough." Then the former managing editor of the *Birmingham* (Alabama) *News* grinned.

"When a reporter handed me a story," he said, beginning to pace, "I knew what was wrong with it and I fixed it! I tore it to shreds!" Stallworth picked up a copy of the local newspaper and ripped it into long, ragged strips.

"And they hated me for it!" he thundered, wadding the torn shreds of paper into a ball.

He kept grinning as he described his conversion from hard-bitten editor who "fixed" copy to hard-driving coach who helped reporters improve their own copy and, in the process, become better writers. He continued working the wad of newsprint as he talked.

"The copy isn't what it's all about," he said, his eyes moving from face to face in the audience. "The *reporter's* what it's all about."

His eyes settled on an especially skeptical editor, who had been leaning back in his chair, arms folded, head tilted.

"How long do your reporters stay with you?" Stallworth asked.

Uncomfortable at being singled out, the man shifted in his chair. "Eighteen months, maybe," he answered. Around the room, heads nodded.

"You just get 'em broke in good," Stallworth said, "and you gotta start all over with a new one, right?"

"Well, yeah," the editor agreed.

"You know why your reporters leave you?"

The editor shrugged. "The pay stinks," he said, provoking laughter and more nodding around the room.

"The pay stinks everywhere," Stallworth said. "Reporters leave you because they aren't learning anything from you. They aren't getting any better. Keep teaching them and they'll stay longer."

Still gently kneading the wad of newsprint, Stallworth explained the difference between an editor and a coach.

"The editor takes the copy from the reporter and fixes it. The story then belongs to the editor, not the reporter. The editor stays mad at the 'stupid' reporter, and the reporter stays mad at the 'pigheaded' editor.

"The coach sits down with the reporter and asks two questions: 'What's good about this story?' and 'How could it be better?' By the time the reporter answers those questions, she's ready to fix the story herself. She's learned how to write better, and the story is still hers. She's proud of it.

"Instead of being ripped up, the story comes out whole," Stallworth concluded. Then he carefully opened up the ball of newspaper he'd been holding. It had been restored to a full page.

"There's nothing magic about it," he concluded, the grin splitting his face. "It's just plain common sense."

Coaching: Definitions and Distinctions

Coaching is a relatively new profession and skill set, and as such, there's sometimes confusion about what it is and isn't. According to the International Coach Federation (ICF), *coaching* is "partnering with clients in a thought-provoking and creative process that inspires them to maximize their personal and professional potential." Coaching is about creating a positive path forward: it focuses on the future (not the past, unless to learn from it). Coaching focuses on what the client *wants*, not what he or she doesn't want (the key of the Law of Attraction).

Solution-focused coaching is about creating the optimal outcome to an issue or moving forward to craft a new opportunity. Coaching isn't necessarily about "fixing" a problem—it can be brought into play when a person has a lofty goal or pet project that hasn't been implemented yet, or wants to grow and explore more of his or her potential.

> **KEY TERM**
>
> **Coaching** Partnering with clients in a thought-provoking and creative process that inspires them to maximize their personal and professional potential.

Obviously, as a manager or business leader, you aren't expected to be a "pure" coach. "Coach" is probably just one of many hats you wear. We know you probably aren't a professional coach and *only* a coach. As you read through this chapter, keep your personal role in mind. You'll be able to tell when the information presented is truly relevant and where it should be adjusted to fit your situation.

Good coaching makes a few key assumptions about clients. Coaches should respect the client's worldview, treat them as whole and absolutely all right as they are, perceive them as resourceful, and chal-

> **TOOLS**
>
> **ICF**
>
> The ICF is the world's largest organization for coaches. The group is dedicated to advancing the coaching profession with high standards, independent certification and credentialing, and a global network of credentialed coaches. Their Web site is found at www.coachfederation.org, and you can find credentialing information, research articles, accredited training programs, and many more resources.

lenge them in playing a "bigger game" and taking a big-picture view. Coaches help clients find the answers and resources within themselves, essentially unlocking their internal genius. Clients who specifically seek coaching will get the most out of it if they are ready to *work* for a change (chronic complainers generally don't want to work for a change, they just want to vent or get validation). They look for coaching because they want to move forward and grow beyond what they currently are without being told they are "broken" or "need fixing."

WORK WITH THE WILLING

Be aware of how you provide coaching to your employees. Not everyone is coachable—you have to work with the willing. A person who only wants to complain or is invested in being a "victim" may not respond to coaching techniques and in fact may resent the attempt. Gauge their responses carefully and make note of who responds to coaching and who doesn't.

DRAWING THE LINE

CAUTION

Be careful that you don't end up trying to "fix" a person or provide therapy if there's a serious problem. Issues such as clinical depression, relationship problems, mental disorders, medical issues, illegal activity, and so on won't respond to coaching, and coaching isn't appropriate in these cases. Know when to refer someone to an Employee Assistance Program or other outside help. Be aware of the limits of what you can offer and where other help is available.

Distinctions

Coaching is *not* the same as therapy, mental health services, counseling, guidance, mentoring, teaching, training, or advising. It may overlap some of these areas and can certainly be used in conjunction with them, but it's not a replacement for these helping techniques. Coaching is *not* appropriate for every situation and person (some just won't respond). Luckily, as a manager, you have a lot of other resources for supporting your employees that can be used in conjunction with coaching.

Coaching differs from therapy and counseling in that it tends to focus on the present (to get a snapshot) and the future (to create new possibilities). Coaching is less worried about the past (except to learn from it) and the *why* of something, and focuses more on the *how* to move forward. Coaching treats clients as whole and resourceful, exactly as they are. Counseling and therapy are important ways to help people resolve issues that may have roots in the past, where the "why" of it needs to be explored, where it may result in crisis mode, and where the person is not well. Coaching won't help a person in mental or emotional crisis and should not be used in this case.

Coaching may seem similar to mentorship and giving advice, but there are some subtle differences. A professional coach does not only offer advice or tell a person to follow a certain path. A coach might offer options, which the client can then choose whether or not to take up and commit to. A coach treats the client as an expert in his or her life, and thus fully capable of creating a path and following it. A coach elicits responses from the per-

> **WHY VS. HOW**   SMART
>
> When something goes wrong in the workplace, instead of asking *why* it happened (which can lead to blaming, shaming, and a lot of finger-pointing), ask *how* it happened (and look at processes, procedures, roles, and work flow).
>
> MANAGING

son, rather than providing "easy answers." Mentorship can be very valuable in the workplace because mentors may also be experts in the same field as the mentoree, or can offer personal insights and advice a coach wouldn't have. Giving advice can be appropriate in the workplace, but it's not the same thing as coaching.

Characteristics of a Good Coach

A good coach is positive, enthusiastic, trusting, focused, sees the big picture, and is observant, respectful, patient, clear, curious, and objective. Let's look at how these characteristics come into play in the workplace.

A good coach is *positive*. Your job when coaching is *not* correcting mistakes, finding fault, and assessing blame. Instead, your function is achieving goals by coaching your staff to peak performance. Focusing on the positive means that you start with what's good and what works, and spend your attention and energy there. When you encourage the positive, you put more attention on it, and your staff will respond in kind.

Mark knows he is supposed to complete his monthly service reports by the fifth. Even though the process is done by online form and seems quick, he is the only IT tech to be consistently late—he usually submits his reports around the 10th. Although he's been encouraged and then warned about getting them in on time, he still seems to lag behind.

Instead of reprimanding him, try a positive approach. It's the difference between saying, "Get those reports in by the fifth *or else*" and asking, "What do you need to do differently to get the reports in on time?"

The first statement reaps resentment and excuses, but no improvement in performance. You continue thinking of Mark as a problem; he goes on thinking of you as a jerk.

THE POSITIVE APPROACH

FOR EXAMPLE Here's how you might try a more positive approach with Mark.

You: We really need those service reports by the fifth. I know that's been difficult for you sometimes, so I'd like to discuss how we can work together to get them in on time.

Mark: I know that the others do them on time. But here's the problem: although the form is online, it seems hardly anyone uses it to request a service call. I mostly just get e-mails or frantic phone calls that someone needs something fixed, and I have to drop everything and go take care of it. I really hate having to re-create the thing on the form later, and that's where I get tripped up. I put it off, I admit, and then I have to remember what happened with minimal notes or e-mails to reconstruct it.

You: What would it take for you to get them done by the fifth?

Mark: For one thing, if everyone else would use the forms properly, it would really help me out. Then I just have to update with the details.

You: I can probably send a reminder memo out about that. What can *you* do about the forms?

Mark: You know, I just heard Todd tell someone on the phone that he was on his way to fix their problem, and that they should start filling out that form as he was on his way. I liked that—maybe I'll try it!

You: Sounds good! Now how about taking the time you need to finish the updates to the files? How might you find that time?

Mark: Hm, I don't know. If I did a little each day, I would probably stay on top of it. It's just that I don't like to do it, frankly, and it always seems small enough to put off until later.

You: I understand—sometimes these things pile up faster than you realize! You should see my filing pile some days! [*both chuckle*] I want you to know that these reports, although they seem tedious, really help us track expenses, as well as who is working on what and for how long. This information factors in how we decide to upgrade appropriately, when to hire more IT folks, where to invest our IT budget, and of course, promotions and raises.

Mark: Really? I didn't know that.

You: Yeah, the information is pretty key. That's why we like to have it by the fifth. It keeps us up to date in a rapidly changing area—we have to make a lot of decisions on limited time frames, so the service reports help back us up.

Mark: I see. Well, you know, I just started something that I do every day: I review my calendar for at least five minutes. I do this at the end of the workday, and it really helps me feel prepared for the next few days. I could add another 10 to 15 minutes to this time to update any forms that need it each day. Oooh!! [*he jumps as a new idea occurs to him*] I could also add an alarm to my calendar around the first of the month to get cracking on those reports, with daily reminders!

You: Strong ideas, Mark! I'll look forward to hearing how these work for you—and seeing your report on the fifth!

Mark: You got it!

Note: As you read through the rest of the qualities of a good coach, see how many of them you can spot at work in this example.

The second approach can get you what you want—the reports turned in on time. And you've got a shot at winning a bonus—a worker with a more cooperative attitude and improved task management skills to work with.

A good coach is *enthusiastic*. As a coach/leader, you set the tone. Your attitude is catching. Project gloom and doom, and you'll get gloom and doom back from your staff. If you concoct reasons why things won't work out, your staff will never disappoint you—things won't work out.

Bring positive energy to every encounter. *Don't* play it cool. Your staff will respond in kind, with some practice.

A good coach is *trusting*. Do you expect workers to be infallible, performing their jobs on time, every time, with no errors?

Of course you don't. Everybody makes mistakes sometimes. Employees have personal crises that interfere with their work. They have

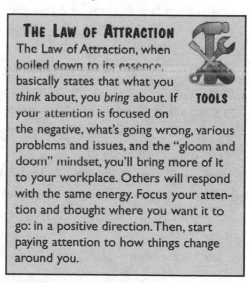

THE LAW OF ATTRACTION
The Law of Attraction, when boiled down to its essence, basically states that what you *think* about, you *bring* about. If your attention is focused on the negative, what's going wrong, various problems and issues, and the "gloom and doom" mindset, you'll bring more of it to your workplace. Others will respond with the same energy. Focus your attention and thought where you want it to go: in a positive direction. Then, start paying attention to how things change around you.

TOOLS

good days and not-so-good days, times of peak efficiency and times when they slide into a stupor. Your staff members are human, a characteristic you share with them.

Do you trust employees to be conscientious, tell the truth, and give a reasonable day's work for a day's pay? You had better. You shouldn't hire

> **TRUST BUT VERIFY**
>
> **CAUTION**
>
> Don't confuse "trusting" with "gullible." You'll have your share of behavior problems, personnel conflicts, and even incompetence to deal with. (That's why you get paid the big bucks, right?) Just don't automatically assume the negative. You should side solidly with the workers until and unless they give you compelling reason not to.
>
> When there's a problem, work with the employee to correct it. You'll wind up with a better employee—and a loyal one, too.

someone unless you're willing to extend that kind of trust. Most people are conscientious and honest, with an inherent desire to do their jobs well. When they see you applying high standards to your own conduct, they'll be even more likely to do the same. Tell them what to do, and then let them do it. Don't let them catch you looking over their shoulders.

A good coach is *focused*. The temptation can be overwhelming. While you've got the employee in your office discussing current performance, why not discuss the other problems you've been meaning to tackle for weeks?

Don't do it. Don't take that poor worker on a guided tour of your personal Hall of Horrors.

Effective coaching is specific and focused. Deal in particulars. Keep the task manageable. Keep the conversation focused on the issue at hand, and don't let it devolve into a gripefest or a venting session. You're far more likely to get action if that employee leaves your office focused on resolving the issue at hand.

A good coach *sees the big picture*. "Why does she want me to do that?" If you leave workers pondering that question after you've explained an assignment, you've only done half the job. You've given them the "what" but not the "why."

Base your assignments on clear, definable goals. Tie specific tasks to those goals. Communicate those goals to the people who actually have to do the work. Help your employees see how their work contributes to the goal, the team, the department, the company, the bottom line, and the overall mission.

Many of us can get blinded by what is happening right in front of us and forget to take a larger view. A good coach can help a person do this. A great analogy for this is that of a football game. If you're low in the stands, you can only view what is happening right in front of you. From there, it's harder to see what's going on in the end zone or the whole field. A coach can encourage a person to "rise up," maybe all the way to the skybox, to take in a larger view of the game and all its components.

FROM SKYBOX TO BLIMP

TOOLS

You can and should help someone take the skybox view of their game of life or work. Try going for the "blimp" view—in which the person can see beyond just the game to the stadium (team), town (department or company), and beyond. You can go even higher—some call this the 30,000-feet-altitude view (as if from the window of an airplane). At this "height," people can get a *really* big picture of how their actions impact the world at large.

A good coach is *observant*. A few years back, Tom Peters made "management by walking around" a corporate litany. It's not good enough, he noted, to sit in your office, even if your door is "always open." You need to get out and mingle with the troops.

Fair enough. But wherever you are, you need to pay attention.

Being observant means more than just keeping your eyes and ears open. You need

BE OBVIOUSLY OBSERVANT

CAUTION

Don't hide your talents. That's generally good advice, of course. What we mean here is that employees should know that you're observant, that you're paying attention. When they're talking to you, maintain eye contact. You might want to take notes. Don't do anything else while they're talking. When you're out and about in the work area observing, make sure employees know you're there. Nobody likes a spy.

to be aware of what *isn't* said as well as what *is*, picking up on body language and tone of voice. Listen to your intuition as well—your gut might alert you when something needs attention.

If you're paying attention, you won't have to wait for somebody to tell you about a problem. You'll see it coming—and may be able to head it off.

A good coach is *respectful*. Respect everybody around you. Respect their rights as employees and as human beings. This can be as simple as avoiding assumptions or cutting someone a little slack, perhaps over-looking a snappish retort from a worker who's tired and stressed from a deadline. It can be as complex as learning that a gesture you make frequently to indicate approval comes across as demeaning to someone from another culture.

A good manager tries to learn everything that might matter to the business and then applies that knowledge. Well, your employees certainly matter, so you should learn who they are and treat them all as individuals, with respect. A good coach also respects the client's worldview. After all, the employee is the expert in his or her own life. When you respect that point of view and make it obvious, the worker will feel empowered, validated, and more engaged.

Along with respect can follow *empathy*. Being empathetic with your employees lets them know that you see them as human. It helps them feel not so alone. However, be sure you don't cross the line into sympathy or pity. Feeling sorry for someone else doesn't do much to help them, and it leaves you with an emotional burden.

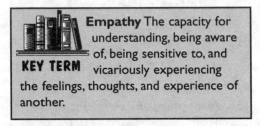

Empathy The capacity for understanding, being aware of, being sensitive to, and **KEY TERM** vicariously experiencing the feelings, thoughts, and experience of another.

A good coach is *patient*. "How can they be so stupid?!" you wail. "I've told them and *told* them!"

Patience, friend. It isn't just a virtue—it's a survival skill in the workplace. Your workers aren't stupid, and they aren't trying to drive you crazy. They're busy, and they're preoccupied, just as you are. It could also be that they're ignorant, which is quite different from being stupid. Ignorance is curable, and you've got the medicine they need—information and a bigger perspective.

Tell them again, but find other words to do so. Using a new approach, ask them to explain the issue to you, as if you were a new worker (a role reversal that will help them think and see differently). That will show that they understand your directions, and it will help them internalize those directions. Remember the old saying, "To teach is to learn twice."

You can't change people, they have to change *themselves*. Their timeline for change and growth is probably quite different from your own. Don't expect them to change overnight. Don't measure everyone by the same yardstick.

A good coach is *clear*. If they didn't hear you right, maybe it's because you didn't say it right. Maybe you just thought you did.

Everybody has seen it happen. The characters and the setting may vary widely, but the scenario is basically the same: I explain something to you, but you don't understand, so I repeat it, using essentially the same words, only *louder* or more s-l-o-w-l-y. The scenario continues, with everyone getting frustrated, angry, and further apart.

Whose fault is it? Yours for not understanding? Or mine for failing to find a more effective way to communicate? It doesn't matter whose "fault" it is. You and I are not connecting.

Here's the bottom line: If you're trying to communicate and the other person doesn't understand, take responsibility for making the connection. Above all, don't make matters worse by repeating the same words louder or more slowly.

A good coach will reiterate what the client says, word for word, and even ask "Have I got that right?" to be sure both are on the same page. If the worker seems unclear on what is going to happen next, a good coach will ask her to state it back as she understands it.

A good coach is *curious*. When you coach someone, a genuine curiosity serves you well. It will make the questions you ask more authentic (instead of "leading" the person to a particular, expected answer). When you are curious, you open the doors to more possibilities, which can elicit more from the employee. If you say, "I'm just curious, what might happen if . . ." you offer a way for the employee to dream a bit without the fear of having a "right" or "wrong" answer. The person's natural resourcefulness starts to come forth. Not every idea will be actionable or implementable, of course, but it broadens the pool of possibilities. Being curious keeps your own mind open to possibilities you might not have thought of.

A good coach is *objective*. When coaching, especially in the workplace, stay objective as much as possible. Professional coaches don't express judgment (disapproval or approval) or opinions—a manager *is* expected

COACH'S QUESTIONS

TOOLS

One of the keys to effective coaching is asking questions rather than providing answers (see Chapter 5). The specific questions, and the order in which you ask them, make the difference between success and failure. Here's an effective one-two punch for many situations: (1) What's good about it? (2) How could it be better?

This approach stresses the positive, expresses curiosity, is respectful of the employee's knowledge, and encourages a strong response. Questions like these build on the work's strengths, rather than focusing on any weaknesses. Can the person who just finished the work really analyze its strengths and weaknesses? Absolutely. Nobody knows them better.

to do so when appropriate, however. If you stay objective when coaching, the employee will be encouraged to do so as well.

You can still be positive and enthusiastic while being objective; it just takes practice. Be positive and enthusiastic about the person or the business. A good coaching session focuses on the *client's* (or employee's) agenda, not your own, although as a manager you may set the topic to talk about (behavior, performance).

Being a good coach doesn't mean you're passing on your managerial responsibility to make decisions. It means you're making sure that you understand what's involved in any decision, that you can communicate

TIME FOR A TEST

Now for a quick reckoning. Take a few minutes to rate yourself on each of the 11 attributes of a good coach. For each characteristic, rate yourself using this scale: 5 (always), 4 (frequently), 3 (50/50), 2 (rarely), or 1 (never).

Characteristic	Rating				
Positive	5	4	3	2	1
Enthusiastic	5	4	3	2	1
Trusting	5	4	3	2	1
Focused	5	4	3	2	1
Sees the big picture	5	4	3	2	1
Observant	5	4	3	2	1
Respectful	5	4	3	2	1
Patient	5	4	3	2	1
Clear	5	4	3	2	1
Curious	5	4	3	2	1
Objective	5	4	3	2	1

your decisions effectively, and that your employees are willing and able to act appropriately. That's how you get things done.

How did you do? Obviously, 4s and 5s speak well for you as an effective coach. But too many 5s might indicate that you're dreaming. (Use this reality check: If you asked your employees to rate you anonymously, would your scores be as high?) If you gave yourself some 2s and 1s, you've identified areas for personal growth.

But how can you work on being more positive or observant, for example? These are characteristics, after all. You've either got them or you don't, right?

Wrong. That's a little like saying either you're born knowing how to do long division or you aren't. Some people take to long division more readily than others, just as some have an easier time mastering a language or making a balky computer behave. You've already learned how to do hun-

---

SPECIFICITY MATTERS

You told Susan that you needed a particular evaluation "as soon as possible," and you understood which evaluation you meant and that "as soon as possible" meant by the end of the day.

When Susan heard this request, she had six other evaluations sitting on her desk in various stages of completion. She didn't ask for clarification because she didn't want to look stupid and make you lose that famous temper of yours. She assumed "as soon as possible" meant as soon as she got finished with the four other projects you dumped on her that morning.

When you didn't have the evaluation by the next morning, you got mad at Susan. After you were done chewing her out, the feeling was mutual. Here's a way to avoid the problem.

1. Think through exactly what you want done and when you want it.
2. Say what you want, very specifically. Be exceptionally clear.

You: Can you finish the Tyler evaluation by the end of the day?

Susan: Do you want me to do that before I finish the estimate for the Marler job?

You: I forgot about that. No. You'd better do the Marler job first.

Susan: Even if I can't get to Tyler today?

You: Right.

Susan: No promises, but I might be able to finish both.

You: That would be fantastic. How can I help with that?

> **Susan:** Maybe if someone took my calls for a while, I could have more time to focus on both.
>
> **You:** In that case, I'll ask Len to cover your phone.
>
> Susan comes away with clear directions, and you have reasonable expectations. You've put her in a win–win position: If she gets the estimate done promptly, even though it means putting the evaluation off until tomorrow, she meets the performance goal the two of you established. If she catches a prevailing wind and gets both done, she exceeds expectations.

dreds of difficult things. You can learn how to develop your coaching attributes, too.

Translating Attitudes into Actions

In the movie *As Good as It Gets,* at a crucial point in his on-screen relationship with Helen Hunt, the waitress he is ineptly trying to woo, the obsessive-compulsive romance novelist played by Jack Nicholson comes up with what he hopes will be a good enough compliment to prevent her from walking out on him: "You make me want to be a better man."

It is, she admits, the best compliment she's ever received. She knows she's important to him because she inspires him to improve.

In real life, can you learn to be more patient, supportive, clear, and assertive? Sure. You can *choose* your attitude—if being a better manager matters enough to you. As with most other tasks, you learn by doing—one trait at a time, using positive visualization and at least a three-week trial period.

Interested? Here's how to do it.

FORMING A NEW HABIT

TOOLS

If you want to make a change in your life—from trying something new to improving your attributes and skills— give yourself enough time for the change to take hold. Research shows that new habits are formed after 21 to 30 days of daily practice. That's right—at least three weeks before you go from "effort" to "habit," when it becomes part of the background of what you do. So if you're experimenting with a new technique or focusing on growing your skills, stick with it for at least a month and then judge whether you want to keep up with it.

Pick an attribute from the list for which you gave yourself a score of 3 or lower. For this example, we'll assume you picked "patient." Develop a clear mental picture of what you look like and how you act when you're being patient. Visualize it as if you're looking into the mirror and seeing the patient you. You don't want an idealized picture of how the Perfect Boss acts. See *yourself* in the role.

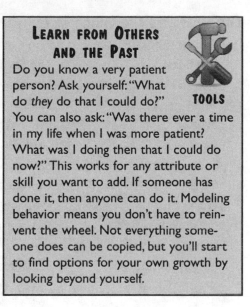

LEARN FROM OTHERS AND THE PAST

Do you know a very patient person? Ask yourself: "What do *they* do that I could do?" **TOOLS** You can also ask: "Was there ever a time in my life when I was more patient? What was I doing then that I could do now?" This works for any attribute or skill you want to add. If someone has done it, then anyone can do it. Modeling behavior means you don't have to reinvent the wheel. Not everything someone does can be copied, but you'll start to find options for your own growth by looking beyond yourself.

Mentally imagine your most aggressive employee in a highly combative situation. See yourself handling the situation effectively and, above all, patiently.

If you're doing a good job of visualizing the scenarios, you may feel yourself getting angry. That's normal. Take several deep, cleansing breaths, and continue working through the scenario, maintaining your focus on patience. What are you doing differently to be more patient? What are the results?

Replay the scene while you brush your teeth, drive to work, or wait for somebody's voice mail system to kick in. When you feel confident that you've grown in the art of being patient, put your visualization into action. The next time you find yourself in a confrontation, bring out your best, most patient self.

This doesn't mean that you're repressing your true feelings. You're in touch with exactly how angry and exasperated you are. You just aren't acting on or engaging with those feelings. Instead, you're acting with patience.

To see how much you've grown in patience, on the next page, rank yourself again on that 1–5 scale and see how you've changed from before you started.

The Boss and the Coach: A Comparison

Here's how the traits of a boss compare with those of a coach.

The Boss	The Coach
Talks a lot	Listens a lot
Tells	Asks
Fixes	Prevents
Presumes	Explores
Seeks control	Seeks commitment
Orders	Challenges
Works on	Works with
Puts product first	Puts person first
Wants reasons	Seeks solutions
Assigns blame	Takes responsibility
Keeps distant	Makes contact

In a sentence, the coach lets the players play the game.

Seeing Yourself as Others See You

This suggestion is for the brave: Ask someone to hold a mirror up so you can see yourself in action.

The person who serves as your reflector must be observant, articulate, and secure enough to tell you the truth. And you have to be ready to hear that truth—and act on it.

SMART MANAGING

ATTITUDE YIELDS ATTRIBUTE

Assume the attitude, and you *will* develop the attribute. Sounds simple, but it works. Put on the attitude that you already *are* patient (positive, enthusiastic, trusting, and so on), and your actions will flow from that state of mind naturally.

Explain to this person that you want her to pay attention to your interactions for the next three weeks. Describe the specific behavior you're trying to change and what you hope to accomplish. Then ask for frequent feedback.

Bringing a reflector into the process can provide two important benefits: (1) you get useful information, in the form of a description of your behavior from an outside perspective, and (2) you've increased your investment by adding accountability. You're a lot more likely to work on your behavior after you've told somebody what you're doing.

The Coach's Checklist for Chapter 2

☑ Review the definition of coaching and how it differs from other roles in the workplace, like mentoring, counseling, therapy, teaching, training, and advising.

☑ Evaluate the attributes of good coaches: A coach is positive, enthusiastic, trusting, focused, sees the big picture, and is observant, respectful, patient, clear, curious, and objective.

☑ Follow these steps to develop the traits of a good coach: (1) tackle one trait at a time and learn how to translate it into action, (2) give yourself a chance to make mistakes and learn from your experience, and (3) give yourself enough time to gain competence.

☑ Choose someone to be a reflector, someone who can help you see yourself as others see you. Then learn from what this person tells you to improve your coaching skills.

What Do Your Players Want?

Being a conductor is kind of a hybrid profession because most fundamentally, it is being someone who is a coach, a trainer, an editor, a director.

—Michael Tilson Thomas

As I started as a shy young conductor, I always wanted to cooperate. To build up the musicians. To help them to be better than without a conductor. And sometimes young talented musicians have to be encouraged.

—Kurt Masur

This book is for and about you, the manager. But there's another side of the story—the players. You can't do much without them.

Imagine a symphony orchestra. It's a large group, made up of violins, violas, cellos, bass, percussion, woodwinds, brass, and sometimes more instruments. At any given concert, there might be a few featured soloists or a whole chorus performing, or a ballet as well. There's an audience, waiting to experience something exciting and beautiful.

In front of the players, with his back to the audience, is the conductor. The conductor is responsible for getting the best performance out of the players. If he's done his job well, he's coached them over the previous weeks of rehearsals, so that their skills are sharp and their knowledge of the music is strong. He steers the ship, while the players make it move. What is created is synergistic—more than just notes sounding separately, *music* flows into the concert hall.

Looking Beyond the Paycheck

To switch metaphors from music to sports (although much of the following applies to professional musicians and other performers), professional athletes play, even when in pain, for three fundamental reasons.

1. The so-called salary drive explains why some not only play but play their best even in "meaningless" games, long after championships have been decided. They're trying to collect impressive statistics to bring to their next contract negotiation.
2. New York Yankees great Joe DiMaggio put the second reason into words when a sportswriter asked him why he continued to play after the Yankees had clinched the pennant. "Because," DiMaggio reportedly said, "somebody might have never seen me play." He knew he was the draw, and he didn't want to disappoint anyone.
3. Most important, athletes are motivated by *pride.* They're the best at what they do, and they want to go out and keep doing it. Even when they are paid millions to play, no matter what their win–loss record is, many of them still crave a championship win.

These three sources of motivation from the world of sports are paralleled in the business arenas. Employees want to earn tangible rewards for good performance, they don't want to disappoint others, and they're proud of what they do. The motives that stem from pride (a positive direction) will move them more powerfully than greed or fear ever could.

Three Drives That Motivate Your Staff

Look around at the people with whom you work every day. From the biggest go-getter to the person who just seems to be putting in time, all are motivated to some extent by three strong forces that get them up in the morning when nothing else will:

1. the desire to achieve

2. the burn to learn
3. the craving to contribute

Let's consider what each of these motivators can teach you about how to coach for peak performance in the workplace.

The Desire to Achieve

Low self-esteem has become something of a generic diagnosis of choice for poor performance these days. To cure low self-esteem, experts have prescribed praise, and lots of it. That seems to be a good idea, in principle. But there's a problem: *Indiscriminate* praise doesn't work as a reward. If everybody gets it, praise has no value. Praise and rewards, by their very nature, must discriminate among levels of performance.

That's not to say that self-esteem isn't important to performance. The better an employee feels about himself and his abilities, the more likely he is to perform well. It is incredibly satisfying to know you have done a good job on something. How-

PAY ATTENTION

Note well what we have to say about rewards here. It explains why across-the-board merit raises and the like are at best a contradiction and at worst a hoax. We take up the subject of rewards in detail in Chapter 14.

ever, if he is not confident about his skills, he will be more hesitant to stretch forward and take risks, just playing it safe and taking any failure or setback deeply to heart as "proof" of being not worth very much.

So higher self-esteem can result in better performance. What can a coach do to promote self-esteem?

This question answers itself if we substitute a new term for "self-esteem." Let's talk, instead, about *mastery.*

Mastery comes from what you can do and how you do it, not what people say about what you can do. You *achieve* mastery; nobody can give it to you—or take it away from you.

People do things, in part, because they *can* do them. Doing them feels good. They continue to do them because they feel themselves getting even better.

Here's an example. Seventh-grade typing class was the first place I distinguished myself in school. I won the ice cream cup most Fridays for typing faster and more accurately than anybody else in class. (There was only *one* ice cream cup prize. Not only was the ice cream good, it was meaningful!)

> **Mastery** Skill, knowledge, and ability that flows naturally and almost effortlessly. To master a task is to be able to undertake it with both competence and confidence. **KEY TERM**

It wasn't really the grade or even the ice cream that motivated me. (I wanted to get good grades in my other classes, too, but that fact alone didn't guarantee success.) It certainly wasn't the fear of failure and the even greater fear of looking like an idiot.

I typed simply for the joy of mastering the skill. That is one of the best feelings in the world.

Achieving mastery takes several steps, which we cover here briefly. If you know these steps, you can measure your own path to mastery, as well as assess where your employees are in their growth.

1. Formulation. Before this stage, a person is not aware that there might be an area for growth. When she decides to learn a new skill, she *formulates the idea*. This is the notion that starts her on the path toward mastery. Until you know that you need or want a change, it won't happen on its own!

For example, let's say that Sharon has to give presentations at work fairly frequently. She's comfortable with researching material and creating PowerPoint slides, but she really doesn't like the speaking part. She gets nervous, and people don't seem to pay attention to her. After getting feedback from coworkers and her manager, she decides that she wants to increase her public speaking skills.

2. Concentration. In the *concentration* phase, a person puts a lot of effort in learning and growing. Perhaps she sets aside time to learn and practice the new skill or ability. At this stage, the learner is really putting in a lot of effort, but probably not getting much return. This phase begins with *high* concentration (putting in a lot, hardly getting any return), and then gradually shifts to low concentration (putting in less effort, getting more of a return).

SMART MANAGING

STAGES OF MASTERY

Refer to the stages of mastery when assessing how your employees are growing in their skills and abilities. You can use this knowledge to determine how to support them in moving to the next stage, educate them about the process, and provide an objective viewpoint for them.

- Formulation
- Concentration
- Momentum
- Stable Growth
- Mastery

Sharon decides to get a few books on public speaking and to check out a local Toastmasters group, which is dedicated to growing public speaking and leadership skills. She starts going to meetings every week, gets a speaking mentor, and starts developing her first presentations to the club. She reads the public speaking books and finds a few blogs online to check out for more information.

3. Momentum. In the *momentum* phase of mastery, the effort from the concentration phase has dropped, and the learner is getting more return on that effort. Things are building on each other, and the person is gaining confidence and feeling more natural in his use of the skill. This stage starts off with low momentum and then moves to higher momentum with more practice.

Sharon starts getting positive evaluations and compliments after a few months of attending Toastmasters meetings, and her mentor is pleased with her progress. She notices that she no longer shakes or has sweaty palms through her speeches. Her colleagues notice that she connects with them more during her work presentations; her slides are also simpler, and she has a lot more energy when she's talking. Her speeches seem more organized and are easier to follow.

4. Stable Growth. At the *stable growth* stage, the person might seem to "plateau" for a while with high momentum and consistent returns. At this stage, she might seem to be consistently achieving well, but still with some effort. To break out of this stage and leap to the next, there might be a breakthrough moment of some sort.

Sharon has been regularly attending Toastmasters meetings for nine months, earning a few awards and designations along the way as she consistently gives speeches. Management has been impressed with her and

COACHING QUESTION

If you feel stuck in a stage on your way to mastery, or you are supporting an employee who seems to be a bit stagnated, ask some questions that might open up room for change.

TOOLS

- What will it take for you to move to the next level?
- If you already were at the next stage, what would you be doing differently than you are now?
- What's *one step* you could take to start moving up the ladder toward mastery?

asked her to write some articles based on her presentations, which she enjoys doing and finds easier than before because of her increased communication skills.

Sharon's breakthrough comes when her nephew announces his engagement and asks her to come up with a toast for the wedding. She surprises herself when she readily accepts, with no fear, only anticipation, and she's already thinking of what to say to express her love and joy for the happy couple.

5. Mastery. After the breakthrough, a person reaches a state of *mastery*. In this state, actions in a particular skill or ability simply flow naturally, with little conscious effort. It feels natural to use these abilities, and the person usually enjoys doing so.

After a year and a half, Sharon's confidence in speaking has reached new heights. She received many compliments on her wedding toast, and she continues to excel at her work presentations. Her manager has asked her to run meetings in his absence, now that she can confidently control the floor and direct the communications, keeping everyone on task. She gets a raise at her performance review because she has demonstrated her willingness to learn and grow, in a way that supports the whole department and company. She starts actively seeking more opportunities to speak in her community and professional groups.

The Burn to Learn

Children are born with an innate drive and ability to learn. The amount of information they absorb before ever starting school is enormous. Western education overlays a strict structure and grade system that can often choke the joy out of learning for many students.

Achievers learn in school to work for the external reward of the grade (and thus, a higher GPA and perhaps better chance of going on to a good college). In fact, many lose the capacity to understand whether they've performed well unless somebody tells them so. This can really throttle the desire to learn, as people begin to wonder "why bother?" if they don't get a grade (or don't get a good one). Also, students naturally become focused on *getting a good grade* (or doing well on a standardized test) rather than on *learning something*.

The underachievers are also damaged by grades. They learn to hate grades, teachers who hand out grades, standardized tests, and the kids who do well. Some learn to actively resist learning anything—even by accident, even for their own good.

FOR EXAMPLE

BURN TO LEARN

Have you ever seen a four-year-old boy learn about dinosaurs (or trucks, or superheroes)? It's downright inspiring to watch a child find something fascinating and then devote a lot of time to wanting to learn more. Books, movies, TV shows, toys, and models will fill his time as he absorbs all kinds of information. He can pronounce difficult words like "Deinonychus" and "Triceratops" flawlessly and will endlessly explain details on these creatures while acting out how they lived, fought, and died. A few years later, in school, when he's asked to write a report about the Cretaceous era, he drags his feet because he has learned to dread writing for grades and the stress of deadlines and evaluation.

What's your favorite pleasure read? Some of us pick up *Sports Illustrated* or *People*. Others choose a Danielle Steele or Stephen King novel. A few may cozy up to Dostoyevsky in the original Russian. Whatever you read, when you're reading what you love, you don't have any problem paying attention (unless you're really tired). You don't need the threat of an exam or a critical paper hanging over your head to keep you turning the pages. You don't need to take notes to remember what you read. You have an inherent burn to learn.

That kind of motivation isn't just for kids. We keep it through the years, although it may get lost in the shuffle of a standardized education system. That's important for you to keep in mind, as both a person and as a manager.

Beyond grades, beyond paychecks and performance reviews, beyond any external motivation you can create, the burn to learn alone can move your staff to new heights.

The Craving to Contribute

You may have seen a TV ad for TOMS shoes (see www.toms .com). This company, founded in 2006 by Blake Mycoskie, sells shoes, of course, but they go far beyond that. For every pair of new shoes sold, another new pair is donated to a child in need in a developing country. As of September 2010, that added up to over a million pairs of shoes. New shoes lower the risk of soil-transmitted disease and injuries and actually *increase* the chances of a child attending school (where shoes might be required). Mycoskie was moved to start this company after traveling in Argentina and witnessing the poverty and health problems there.

> **LEARNING STYLES**   **SMART**
>
> To fuel your employees' burn to learn, assess their best learning styles. Some do best when "thrown" into a task to **MANAGING** learn by doing. Some do well and learn best if they attend classes, conferences, or meetings. Others prefer online learning, either through self-paced courses or webinars and tele-seminars. Some prefer reading or one-on-one mentorship. Knowing how best to support your employees' learning sets everyone up for success.

In addition to donating shoes, the TOMS mission has caught on with other corporate citizens, inspiring collaborations and more donations. TOMS created and sponsors One Day Without Shoes, a yearly event to raise awareness. There are now Campus Clubs for TOMS shoes, to connect with passionate people with fresh ideas.

How about you? Do you feel that your work contributes to the greater good in some way? Long ago, many people made or grew things, real things that they could hold in their hands—machine parts or a stalk of corn. At the end of the day, they knew what they had done and how well they had done it. Now fewer people know that feeling of satisfaction, as there might be a disconnect between what they do and what the company eventually produces. Some create nothing more tangible than a disk file of data. Those who still work with their hands often perform one or two simple functions, a tiny part of a much larger process, far removed from the final product.

Disk files or printouts are seldom a source of great pride—particularly when they're filed away somewhere (or shredded to make way for the next set of printouts). There's little joy, at the end of the day, in being able to say that you tightened 23,692 bolts, an increase over 23,415 the day before.

Something in us yearns to make a difference. You feel it, the farmer feels it, the cop on the beat feels that craving to contribute—and so does everybody who works with you.

If you can help employees understand the value of what they do and how it contributes to the larger picture, you're helping them achieve peak performance.

Strategies for Motivational Coaching

Motivating another person can be extremely difficult. In fact, it's impossible—you cannot change another person. A person has to feel motivation from *inside*. As a manager-coach, you can help your employees tap into their inner motivation. For each of the three motivators just discussed, there's a corresponding strategy you can apply.

1. To feed the desire to achieve, provide appropriate challenges. Ask them what they want to achieve, personally and professionally. Then, challenge them with tasks that can also meet their personal goals. Here are three simple tips for challenging employees.

- **Let them do the job.** Managers who don't delegate responsibility often make bad bosses. When you assign a goal for workers to reach, also assign the responsibility for achieving it and provide the means for doing it right.

- **Match the worker to the task.** Find out what each worker is good at doing (or wants to learn more about). Plan for success. Keep workers striving to reach the next level of achievement.

> **DELEGATION**
>
> When you delegate something, you should fully entrust the other person to handle it. Delegation is *not* giving someone a task and then hovering around to make sure they do it exactly as you would do it. Trust the other person to handle it, and consider delegation more of a collaborative effort.
>
> MISTAKE PROOFING

- **Focus on *process* as well as *product*.** The journey is as important as the destination. Help employees work through the steps, gaining mastery as they go.

> **ADDED BENEFITS**
>
> TRICKS OF THE TRADE
>
> Notice how, in Sharon's case earlier in this chapter, getting better at public speaking had a lot of other payoffs that she might not have expected. She wanted to get better at it because she wasn't happy with her performance. Along the way, she earned designations and awards through Toastmasters, new responsibilities and rewards at work, and the admiration of her peers and friends.
>
> When motivating your employees, think about asking bigger-picture questions. Say Sam is working on an appropriate challenge and is excited about it. Make it even more worthwhile and more motivating by asking him what *else* might result. Would a successful outcome generate more income (a raise?), a new opportunity (promotion?), increased respect? Would work relationships (or even personal relationships) be improved? Who else would notice or be affected?

2. To serve the burn to learn, create and support learning opportunities.
You might need to shake loose some money for a workshop, training
event, class, or conference, or allow workers the time needed to take
advantage of these opportunities. There are lots of learning opportunities
available. If you know your employees' preferred learning styles, you can
support them as they find what will work best—from conferences,
classes, webinars, tele-courses, professional groups, reading or audio-
books, mentorship, or intensive training.

SMART MANAGING

LET THEM. DON'T MAKE THEM.

You won't have to force
employees to get a job done
when they work from the
need to achieve. Simply create opportunities and an environment in which they
can do good work.

You can also create learning opportunities in the workplace.

Now, you may be think-
ing, "I'm not a teacher!" Fair
enough. But often you won't
need to teach; you'll just need
to get out of the way so they
can learn. Put a challenge, the
necessary resources, and workers together with a clearly defined goal and
stand back. You won't teach them directly—but they'll learn. They might
surprise you, and teach *you* a thing or two! (We examine your role as
trainer in Chapter 8.)

3. To cater to the craving to contribute, give them work that matters. Let
these four simple words guide you as a coach: *Never waste their time.*

Don't assign work just to keep somebody busy, and don't call a meeting simply for the sake of having a meeting. That behavior shows a lack of
respect for your employees—and it's a waste of time for the company.

Here are two tips to help you make sure that the work you assign has
meaning for employees.

Their Actions Have to *Count*

When you ask employees to provide input or make decisions, mean it.
Otherwise, the results may be worse than if you hadn't involved them at
all.

Nobody likes to commit without consequences or work without
results. It's that simple.

LISTENING MATTERS

FOR EXAMPLE

I once served a term on the board of a church grade school. We were under the nominal leadership of the parish pastor, but he never attended our meetings. We put in nine months developing policies regarding tuition and fees for parish and nonparish members. We struggled to be fair and felt the burden of keeping the school solvent. Our group included an accountant and a lawyer, and the discussions were stimulating and informed.

We reached a consensus, drafted our proposals, and presented them to the pastor. A week later, he issued his decision—which had nothing to do with our proposals and essentially ignored what we had done.

I don't think he understood why some of us were very upset at this. I was a volunteer, so I could walk away without jeopardizing my livelihood and the well-being of my family. The people who work with you may not be so lucky.

If employee input doesn't really matter to you, it will show. They may not trust you again—and certainly would be foolish to ever bother trying to give you honest input.

If you tell employees to make a decision, their decision has to stick. You have to stand by it, support it, and do everything you can to make it work.

Until you're ready to make that commitment, don't set up committees and problem-solving groups. They won't do any good—and they could do a lot of damage, because all you'll really allow them to do is point fingers.

They Need to Know *Why*

A phenomenon common to employees at every level in all institutions and organizations, from the man who scrubs the toilets to the one who signs the welcoming message on the annual report: When the going gets really tough, there's a tendency to lose track of the overall goal and narrow your focus to immediate tasks. This is true across businesses and industries, government, higher education, nonprofits, and the media.

If you work at a hospital, your ultimate job is to cure the sick, to prevent the well from getting sick, and to ease the pain of those for whom you have no cure. Every meaningful task performed at that hospital in some way contributes to those goals.

TRICKS OF THE TRADE

MISSION STATEMENT

Do you know your company's (or department's) mission statement? Do your employees? The mission statement provides the big-picture statement of why a company is in business in the first place. When you can connect a worker's tasks and role to the mission statement of the company, then you can easily help them see that overall goal and *why* they do what they do. Even better: Come up with a mission statement for your group alone, and connect it to the overall mission of the organization.

Every worker in every organization needs to understand the ultimate outcome of his or her work. Give workers the big picture, the reason behind the work, the way their labors contribute to the cause. Ask them how they see their own work contributing to that vision. When you do, you link their work to their need to make a difference.

The Coach's Checklist for Chapter 3

☑ Remember the three attributes that drive your employees (and you) to perform at higher and higher levels: (1) the desire to achieve, (2) the burn to learn, and (3) the craving to contribute.

☑ What's the need to achieve about? It's about gaining mastery over abilities so people feel motivated to perform well.

☑ What's the burn to learn about? People want to learn more about what they love. When they love their work, they want to learn more and get better at it.

☑ What's the craving to contribute about? People naturally want to make a contribution. When employees understand the value of what they do (and what the company does), they naturally seek to improve their performance.

☑ Take actions as a coach to activate the three attributes that drive employee performance to get better results.

Chapter
4

The Signs of Good Coaching

Coaching frequently takes place one player at a time. Forget those fiery "Win one for the Gipper!" locker room speeches (or their business equivalent, the motivational meeting). That's not where the heart and soul of coaching really happen. You'll do your most effective coaching one on one, face to face before the game starts.

In this chapter, we discuss some guidelines to help you plan and perfect your coaching technique.

Body Language

Let's take a look at two scenarios that illustrate the positive and the negative uses of body language to send a message.

In the first scenario, Hank hesitates at his boss's office doorway. It has taken nearly all his courage to come this far, and now he's trying to push on for the last couple of feet.

Maureen, his boss, is frowning at her computer screen, as if expecting it to tell her what to do next. She glances up and sees Hank, and the frown deepens.

"If you're busy . . . ," Hank stammers.

"I'm always busy," Maureen says. "Aren't we all? But come on in."

Her gaze lingers on the screen. She leans back in her chair, folds her arms across her chest, heaves a sigh, and says, "What can I do for you?"

The second scenario begins in a similar way. Hank teeters on Maureen's doorstep, as she scowls at her computer screen. Sensing Hank's presence, she looks up. This time she looks him in the eye and smiles.

"If you're busy . . . ," he stammers.

"I'm always busy," she replies, smiling. "Aren't we all? But come on in."

She stands up, comes out from around the desk, and waves toward one of the two chairs facing each other a few feet to the side of the desk. "What can I do for you?" she says.

SMART MANAGING

THE TWO MAUREENS

I'll tell you a little secret about the two Maureens. The second Maureen, who welcomed Hank with her words *and* actions, was no less busy than the first one. She was no less preoccupied, under no less pressure, perhaps even no happier to see him appear unexpectedly at her door. She just acted in a more approachable way. You should, too, if you really want to be an effective coach.

Same words, different body language, and very different outcomes. In the first example, Hank won't feel at ease, and Maureen will probably not hear what she needs to know.

In both versions, Maureen's words indicate that she's okay (if not totally thrilled) with Hank's interruption. In the first scene, her body language contradicts her words, sending the clear message that Hank is intruding on something important. By glancing at her screen, leaning back, and crossing her arms, she sends a clear message that Hank is not a priority, and her whole demeanor is rather "closed" and defensive. In the second version, her actions reinforce her words, expressing her willingness to give Hank time and attention.

Which speaks louder—her actions or her words?

When the two signals are at odds, employees will believe the actions every time. That's because *nonverbal communication* (body language, gestures, expression, tone of voice, etc.) have a powerful impact on any message. Attention may be focused on the words being said, but all those nonverbal cues are subconsciously processed as well. Nonverbal cues effectively communicate emotions, state of mind, and attitudes; are reliable indicators of true feelings; and may even contradict verbal messages. Body language specifically can account for 60–70 percent of your message!

> **Nonverbal communication** Body movement and position, gestures, expression, tone of voice, and any other way to communicate without words.
>
> **KEY TERM**

Hank doesn't feel welcome in the first scenario and as a result, he gets more nervous. He stands little chance of expressing his concerns or asking his questions. In the second version, Maureen has given herself a much better chance to do some unscheduled coaching and gather important feedback. Hank is more relaxed as he sees her commitment to listening to him when she gets up and moves away from her computer, meeting him as an equal on the same side of the desk.

The Benefits of an Open-Door Policy

There are two key reasons why you should welcome the employee who drops in to talk.

The first reason is that the employee gets to say what's on her mind. You want your workers to feel they can talk to you. More important, they need to know you'll listen and pay attention to their concerns and suggestions. Lacking that assurance, they're more likely to feel stifled, frustrated, and perhaps bitter and alienated. Unhappy workers don't do their best work. They'll still express their concerns, of course—to each other, when you're not around, fueling the office grapevine and lowering morale.

> ### WHAT HANK KNOWS
>
> Hank may not be accurate in his perceptions of the job, his performance, other people's performances, Maureen's fairness, or anything else. He is an expert on only two subjects: what he thinks and how he feels.
>
> **CAUTION**
>
> Maureen is well aware of that and may not agree with him on many issues. She shouldn't pretend to agree when she doesn't. Nor should she promise anything she can't or won't do or any outcome she can't or won't deliver.
>
> But she can and should listen and respond honestly. Every employee deserves that attention and respect.

A second key reason for welcoming an employee dropping by is the opportunity you get to hear her concerns or questions.

You want and need to hear what each employee has to say. Gathering information about employees—their attitudes as well as their aptitudes—is fundamental to good coaching. You can't coach them if you don't *know* them.

If you aren't glad to see the employee who drops in to talk, fake it. You read that right. Even if you aren't happy with the interruption, one of your options is to simply act as if you are. Hypocritical? Not at all.

We aren't talking about how you feel. We're talking about being a more effective manager. You need the employee's input, and that employee needs you to be willing to listen, regardless of how you feel. Acknowledge your feelings to yourself, but act on your awareness. Get out of your chair. Work up a smile if you can (at least ditch the scowl). Come out from behind your desk.

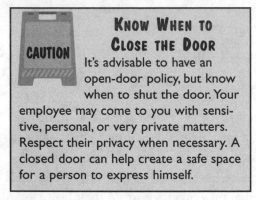

KNOW WHEN TO CLOSE THE DOOR

CAUTION

It's advisable to have an open-door policy, but know when to shut the door. Your employee may come to you with sensitive, personal, or very private matters. Respect their privacy when necessary. A closed door can help create a safe space for a person to express himself.

Don't fake the listening. You must will yourself to focus on what the employee is saying. (You'll often find that easier to do if you get up to greet the person at your door.)

Remember, Hank's no dummy. He can tell that Maureen is busy, and he can usually tell if she isn't happy to be interrupted. He may even expect that, which is why he waited so long to come see her and why he's so nervous about it. But he can also pick up on her willingness to put her work and worry aside, even if she doesn't feel like it. He'll appreciate her for it, because it shows him that he's important to her.

With practice, you can become very convincing and authentic in the role of open, willing listener. Here's the bonus: Your feelings will follow your actions. Act as if you're happy to see that employee who's interrupting your work, and you're apt to feel it, at least a little. Once again, just the physical movements of getting up, moving around your desk, shaking hands, and so forth can really help you get out of your solo mode and into the one-on-one. (See Chapter 6 for more on listening skills.)

If it's really a bad time for an interruption and you can't give the employee your attention now, not even for two minutes, say so. He'll appreciate your honesty, if you handle the situation properly.

There's a good way and a bad way to do this.

If you say, "I'm busy right now. I've got to finish this report for the management meeting," the employee hears (essentially): "Go away. You're not as important to me as the managers."

A better approach is to say, "I'd really like to know what's on your mind, but I need to finish this report for a meeting at 10. How about if I come and find you as soon as the meeting ends, probably about 11, so we can talk then?"

Here's the key: follow your "later" with a "when." If now isn't a good time, set a time that's good for both of you, rather than just leaving it to "whenever."

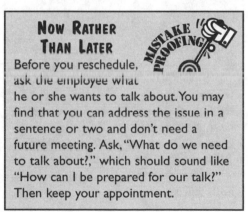

NOT LISTENING: THEY KNOW

SMART MANAGING

If you're not really listening, your employees will be able to tell. They'll sense it at the time, and they'll know for sure later when you fail to act on—or remember—the conversation they thought they were having with you.

If that happens, you may not have to worry about being interrupted again. The employees might not be back. They don't want to waste your time, and they sure don't want to waste their own. Like Hank, they're no dummies.

NOW RATHER THAN LATER

MISTAKE PROOFING

Before you reschedule, ask the employee what he or she wants to talk about. You may find that you can address the issue in a sentence or two and don't need a future meeting. Ask, "What do we need to talk about?," which should sound like "How can I be prepared for our talk?" Then keep your appointment.

"Speaking" Body Language

Imagine that you can't stop talking, no matter how hard you try, and you always say exactly what you feel and think. Jim Carrey made a movie based on this premise (an attorney who can't lie!) and delivered the laughs when his character got into big trouble.

In real life, it wouldn't be so funny, would it?

But consider this—your body "speaks" for you all the time, telling people how you feel and what you think through your expressions, gestures, and posture.

You show apprehension, impatience, displeasure, and disrespect with a tapping pencil and jiggling feet, with shrugs and sighs and scowls. You do, that is, unless you learn to control your body language—just as you've learned to control your tongue.

In the first scenario, Maureen folded her arms across her chest, an indicator of defensiveness and signal of being closed off. She remained seated, a sign of disrespect and unwillingness to be interrupted. She kept a huge prop—her desk—between herself and Hank, presenting a physical as well as a psychological barrier. This set up her visitor as an adversary.

STUDYING HUMAN NATURE

Take a moment from time to time for a nature study—human nature, of course.

The next time you're in a meeting, look around the room. How are people sitting? What are their facial expressions? What gestures are they making? Can you tell if they are engaged or disengaged? If so, how can you tell? Then, ask yourself how those postures, expressions, and gestures make you feel. What do they say about how those people feel?

You can learn a lot by observing the body language around you.

In the second scenario, Maureen stood up, moved out from behind the desk, and invited Hank to sit with her as an equal. (We're assuming that her chair wasn't higher or better than his. If you have two different chairs, offer your guest the better one.) Most important, she made eye contact with Hank, which is the most fundamental way to create an atmosphere for an honest exchange.

By her actions as well as her words, Maureen sent a powerful message of openness and acceptance.

Presenting your own body language appropriately and reading others' body language accurately are good starts. You can use this knowledge to connect with your employees and create rapport when coaching them.

A professional coach knows to match the client's energy—as mentioned elsewhere, this means respecting their worldview, but it also includes matching their vocal tone and body language to a certain extent. Think about it—you're feeling down and out because, say, your beloved dog is sick. Imagine that someone comes at you with a big, cheesy smile and a patronizing request to "turn that frown upside down!" You probably have to fight down the urge to smack that person around.

Matching or closely mimicking an employee's tone of voice and energy level shows that you respect him and where he is emotionally at the moment. When you've gained rapport at that level, a person will start to feel listened to and valued—respected, not dismissed. You can then carefully bring them up to a higher energy level by gradually increasing the energy in your voice. Be aware of whether the person is "coming along with you" and modulate your tone appropriately.

In terms of body language, you can practice *mirroring,* which means that you are essentially mimicking the other person's body language, mirror image. Is she sitting back in the chair, with her legs crossed? You sit the same way. When she leans forward and uncrosses her legs, you might wait a moment or two and then do the same. You don't have to be rigid about it, and you shouldn't appear as if you're mocking the other person (some are sensitive to this, especially if they have a quirky thing they do that no one else does, like twisting their hair around their index finger).

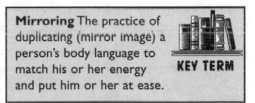

Mirroring The practice of duplicating (mirror image) a person's body language to match his or her energy and put him or her at ease.

KEY TERM

If you have been mirroring your employee's body language for a while, and the rapport is building, you can then start to *lead* the person when you are moving toward action steps and solutions. You are no longer mimicking the other person's actions, you are making your own deliberate body language changes. Chances are good the other person will match you! Lean forward, and they will lean forward; relax a bit and they will relax. You can use this subtle technique to bring them along into higher energy and forward momentum.

The Elements of a Good Coaching Session

To conduct a good coaching session, you need to (1) establish a purpose, (2) establish ground rules, (3) stay focused, (4) avoid monologues,

(5) speak clearly and simply, and (6) stay open to new ideas. Let's look closely at these elements.

Establish a Purpose

In our example for this chapter, Maureen didn't initiate the meeting; Hank did. But she needs to know the agenda, and so would you. The best way to find out is to *ask*.

Your tone of voice is crucial. Use a relaxed, conversational tone with genuine curiosity.

Your words matter, too, of course. If you ask, "What can I do for you?" you assume that you're the one who will do the helping. However, the employee may think that he can do something for you, and maybe he can. If you ask, "So, what's bothering you?" you're sending a negative message with pessimistic expectations. The employee may think that you've labeled him as a malcontent. He might feel hesitant to express what's on his mind.

Keep it simple. "What's up?" or "What brings you here?" will do the job just fine.

If you seek out the employee, the same principles apply, although you wouldn't be asking what they want to talk about if you have a topic of discussion in mind. However, you can still offer an open invitation that will help set them at ease. For instance, you might say, "Keith, let's discuss

SMART

MANAGING

Don't Assume

Don't assume the employee is there to complain. Don't assume he's there because he's angry. And don't assume she's there because she needs something.

He says: "I want to talk about my new assignment."

You assume he means he doesn't like his assignment and ask, "What's wrong with it?"

Now both of you are on the defensive. Chances of a productive conversation are already slim. Let's start over.

He says: "I want to talk about my new assignment."

You make no assumptions. You just say, "Sure. What about it?"

What if you don't remember what his or her new assignment is? (Hey, it happens to all of us. You really are busy and preoccupied, and you've got a lot of people in your department.) Don't bluff. Don't hope to figure it out while he's talking. Ask. Make sure that you're both on the same page from the start.

some opportunities for moving forward" or "Susan, can we have a brainstorming [or debriefing] session on this project?"

Although you might begin the conversation with some social small talk, keep this brief. If that employee is wondering and worrying about the reason for your visit, your attempts at being sociable are likely to increase the curiosity and the discomfort.

Be respectful of their time: "Can you take maybe 15 minutes now? Or would you prefer to set a time for us to meet?"

Establish Ground Rules

The best business meetings (staff meetings, updates, brainstorming) have some sort of agenda and expected rules, even if they aren't in writing. An effective meeting has a clear purpose and protocols (i.e., starting on time, tabling side discussions, whether decisions are made by consensus or majority vote). As with any meeting, you and the employee need to have a common understanding of certain factors when having a one-on-one discussion. The most important factors are time and roles.

USEFUL PROTOCOLS

The military has a tradition of rigid hierarchies that would be inappropriate in a business setting. But you can still learn from military protocol.

When an officer wants soldiers to relax in his presence, he tells them so, quite clearly: "At ease." Then the soldiers know they can move about freely.

When a soldier wants to express something, she makes a request, again quite plainly: "Permission to speak freely, sir?"

Of course, the manager–employee relationship is generally less confining than the officer–soldier relationship. But you can learn from the military that you need to maintain a professional relationship, even in a more relaxed setting or in a one-on-one meeting.

You need to establish a clear time frame for your discussion. If the employee initiates the contact and doesn't ask for a specific amount of time, ask how much he needs or establish the limit yourself. ("I've got a meeting in 10 minutes. Is that going to be enough time? If not, can we meet later, maybe around 3 p.m.?") This respects your time *and* your employee's time. People are busy!

TRICKS OF THE TRADE

CONFIDENTIALITY

A professional coach keeps a client session confidential. In the business world, this isn't always possible for a manager-coach to do. Be clear to your employees if and when you have to report something—for instance, an allegation or admission of illegal activity or suicidal thoughts—to someone else. You are *not* a doctor, therapist, or priest, and you are not bound by confidentiality privilege, even if the employee asks you to keep it to yourself. Be aware of reporting protocols and any company guidelines on when to say something, and be sure your employees know where your obligations and responsibilities lie.

You both need to remember who's the manager and who's the employee. Keep things on a professional basis. You may like your employee as a person, but in the workplace, be clear about separating personal and business roles. Remember: Your job is to *manage* them, not be their friend.

If you don't maintain the manager–employee relationship in a one-on-one meeting, you might wind up with information you can't act on and maybe information you shouldn't even have. You might get inappropriate requests from an employee, which might be viewed as favoritism by others. You might learn things you didn't want to know (gossip) about other workers.

Stay Focused

You'll want to stay focused on the reason for the employee's visit, of course. But there's more involved in keeping focused during the meeting than just listening. Here are a few guidelines.

- **Avoid making "noise."** This is anything that distracts from the atmosphere. As the old song goes, "Every little movement has a meaning all its own." Whatever you do should contribute to the discussion and support your connection with the employee.
- **Don't look at your computer or phone.** Not even once. Turn off the monitor; silence your cell phone or put it out of sight; don't answer your office phone. That will get rid of the temptation to look—and it conveys a clear message to the employee of the importance you place on the conversation.
- **Don't touch your papers.** Again, if you might be tempted, set all papers aside on your desk as soon as you welcome your visitor. One

small action can reduce the temptation and show respect and interest.

- **Don't fidget.** Be aware of any nervous habits you might have and try
to still them. Focusing intently on the other person and putting your
full attention on the topic at hand will help with this.

We come back to these points when we talk about active listening in
Chapter 6.

Another aspect of staying focused is to pay attention to the specific
issue being discussed.

"I've got a problem with the way the office is being run," a worker
challenges you. What's your response?

Let's consider a few possibilities and the advantages and disadvan-
tages of each response, with a little speculation about the likely results.

Option A: "You and me both. What's your beef?"

Pluses: Honest. Down-to-earth. Establishes rapport, empathy, common
ground.

Minuses: Invites a general gripe session.

Probable Outcome: You both complain, and perhaps feel better for having
vented, but you won't be any closer to finding a solution.

Hidden Danger: You'll lose stature in your employee's eyes. It's fine that
you share her sense of outrage, but you're the boss. If you've noticed a
problem, why haven't you done something about it?

Option B: "Really? I thought things were going pretty well."

Pluses: Again, honest and down-to-earth.

Minuses: Establishes a debate. Your worker must now "prove" herself
right—which means proving you, the boss, wrong.

Probable Outcome: You'll shut her up and shut her down. She might
appear to agree with you. But she'll walk away unconvinced and angry.

Hidden Danger: You won't hear from her again. By now you should know
that not hearing from your employees is your problem, not theirs.

Option C: "Yeah? Well, you know what they say: If you aren't part of the
solution, you're part of the problem."

Pluses: Again, engages the issue head-on.

Minuses: Negative and accusatory. Worker has to defend herself. Suggests that anyone who notices a problem better take responsibility for solving it or just keep quiet.

Probable Outcome: Worker shuts up.

Less Likely Outcome: Worker fights back, and you've got an argument. The verbal sparring may be more productive than silence, but it probably won't get you any closer to real understanding or a solution.

Hidden Danger: The dangers here aren't hidden. Nobody could miss them.

Option D: "Hmm."

Pluses: Doesn't lead the conversation or indicate any position. Allows the worker to set the agenda. Indicates you're paying attention.

Minuses: But not much attention. Psychologists get away with this kind of stuff, but it doesn't work as well for managers if a clear response is expected.

Probable Outcome: Your worker may have a tough time getting started without a little help. Or she may feel a need to balance your monosyllabic response by filling out the conversation, which means it might take longer to get to the point.

Hidden Danger: You're seen as passive and noncommittal.

Option E: "What specifically should we talk about?"

Pluses: You put the responsibility for the conversation where it belongs. More important, you've taken the first step toward taking the complaint from general to specific.

Minuses: You might feel that you lose control over the exchange by letting the worker take the lead, but that's a good thing in the world of coaching.

Probable Outcome: The worker will tell you what's really on her mind.

Less Likely Outcome: The worker doesn't really have anything specific in mind and has nothing to say. In that case, you can let a little silence grow. Be patient. It's all right to let her think about it. It's her move.

Option F: "What's the problem? Is it the way the mail gets distributed in the afternoon? I've had a lot of complaints about that. Or do you want to tell me nobody's cleaning out the refrigerator in the break room? Or maybe it's ... "

Pluses: You're concerned and demonstrate awareness.

Minuses: You're giving a multiple-choice test. The worker has to choose from your menu. You may also be bringing up problems she hasn't noticed, which she may then add to her list. You are also putting words in her mouth and making assumptions that may not be accurate.

Probable Outcome: In the best case, the worker will wait you out and tell you what's really on her mind—or try to, anyway. In the worst case, she may feel as though she's just adding to your list of problems and may assume you'll be too busy with the other problems to pay any attention to hers.

Hidden Danger: You thought you were communicating the fact that you're on top of things, but the employee might think you're just throwing up a smoke screen.

Pick Option E for the best coaching opportunity. Or maybe you've got a better option. (Just consider the pluses, minuses, probable outcome, and hidden dangers before you decide that it's better.)

Whatever you do, define the issue and limit the discussion to something manageable. You'll get other chances to discuss other concerns—but only if you resolve this specific concern right now.

Avoid Monologues

Don't launch into a monologue or give a lecture. If you're coaching effectively, your employee should do most of the talking. Have a *conversation*.

This holds true no matter which one of you initiates the session. You're the coach and the employee is the player who can benefit from your guidance. It's generally better for the player to act and the coach to react.

Your job when coaching is to ask questions that elicit the employee's resourcefulness. Offer suggestions only if the person seems truly stuck—and be prepared for the person to choose whether or not to follow the suggestion (he may decide it's not right for him).

Communicate Clearly

Use words that form bridges rather than raise barriers.

Whether you're coaching an employee or meeting with other managers

TRICKS OF THE TRADE

Pass, Play, Counteroffer

A useful tool when offering a suggestion to an employee (if he truly seems stuck on how to move forward) is to present the idea or technique and then ask: "Pass, play, or counteroffer?" This kind of language demonstrates that it's entirely up to the employee to decide whether a suggestion will work for him. You should not be emotionally invested in whether he decides to try it or not. "Pass" means the suggestion is not right for the person. "Play" means she will commit to doing it (and put it on her action list!). "Counteroffer" means it needs a little tweaking and adjusting before she commits to it. This language gives a lot of control to the employee.

or whether you're talking with the man who scrubs the toilets or the woman who chairs the board of directors, these recommendations will help you communicate more effectively.

- Use the simplest, most common terms. Reject terms like "nonfunctional superannuated language equivalents."
- Stow the jargon and the business buzzwords. "Suicide squeeze" doesn't mean anything to someone who isn't a baseball fan. "Leveraging your paradigm for total quality initiatives" is similarly nonsensical.
- Be specific. Which sentence communicates more effectively? "I'm concerned because you've come to work late several times recently" or "Your on-site punctuality modality leaves something to be desired."
- Allow your employee to ask if something seems unclear, or "push back" if the communication isn't obvious. Make sure he understands by asking if it's clear and that you are both on the same page.
- Use the known to explain the unknown. You don't have to be an English major to use metaphor and simile effectively. When you're speak-

CAUTION

Clichés Don't Work

Although comparisons can help people make connections, some of them have been abused and overused, like "level playing field" or "he dropped the ball." Avoid clichés like the plague. (Ouch!)

Also, since business clichés tend to derive from sports and the military, they may cause employees who are unfamiliar with those areas to feel like outsiders. Language that seems exclusionary to an employee will make your work as a coach more difficult. Part of meeting clients "where they are" is respecting their world. Get right in it with them.

ing about something new and/or complex, compare it to something that's familiar to the employee.

I once heard somebody describing how Einstein's theory of relativity explains the possibility of time travel. I actually understood (sort of) what he was talking about, because he compared the Earth's passage through the space-time continuum to a bowling ball rolling on a rubber mat.

THREE TIPS FOR COMMUNICATING

Here are three quick tips for better communication.

1. Narrow the focus to one issue at a time. You'll never get a handle on the way the office is being run. But you might learn that the mail isn't getting distributed until 3 in the afternoon, **TOOLS** and it's affecting customer service.
2. Define the issue clearly. No mystery here. Just make sure you're both talking about the same thing. The person who brings up the issue should be responsible for defining it.
3. Keep it in the present tense, with an eye toward the future. Don't bring up the great system they had where you used to work. Stay with the here and now and bring in a vision of how you *want* it to be.

Be Open to New Ideas

If you talk about "your" idea and "her" idea, you've created two obstacles to finding a solution to the problem. You've limited the discussion to two possibilities, potentially closing the door on a compromise or on a third (or fourth, or fifth) approach.

You're talking about *you vs. her*. The struggle is personal (and one of you has to lose).

You lose either way. If you "give in" and accept the employee's solution, you may feel that you've lost some of your stature as a manager. If you refuse to give ground, and pound your employee into submission, you'll lose any chance of finding a better solution.

Keep the discussion open. Try to disconnect the idea from the person suggesting the idea, so you both feel free to comment, criticize, or modify. You might come up with something neither of you would have thought of alone.

If the worker comes away thinking it was all her idea—so much the

ANOTHER PERSPECTIVE

Broaden the options from "your idea and my idea" to include more perspectives. You

TOOLS could ask questions like "What would someone from a similar company (or a competitor) do? What would your mentor do? What would the CEO do in this situation? Have you ever known someone who was good at this, and what did they do?"

better! That boost in her self-esteem and engagement cost you little or nothing.

Coaching is effective when it's

- one-on-one,
- goal-oriented and focused,
- limited in scope and time,
- conversational, and
- centered on ideas, not personality.

To make your coaching sessions more productive, hone two essential conversational skills—asking effective questions and listening to the answers. We focus on those skills in the next two chapters.

The Coach's Checklist for Chapter 4

☑ Make sure your body language and your words communicate the same message. If not, people will believe what your body says, not your words.

☑ Keep an open door and welcome employees when they come to talk to you—even when you don't feel like it.

☑ Set up and execute a successful coaching session: establish a purpose, establish ground rules, keep focused, avoid monologues, speak clearly and simply, and be open to new ideas.

Asking Good Questions

Everybody knows how to ask good questions, right?

Wrong. In fact, the question you just read isn't very good, because it implies its own "right" answer, the answer you're supposed to give. It's also a trick question because the "right" answer turns out to be wrong.

To illustrate how carefully questions must be worded to get useful information, let's take an example. Let's suppose that, as you're shopping at the mall on a Saturday afternoon, you're approached by a smiling person carrying a clipboard. You're about to be interviewed by an opinion pollster.

Here's the question you're asked: "Do you feel that a person who has been caught engaging in an immoral activity can be trusted to serve in high elected office?"

Your opinions about politicians and public servants really aren't the issue here. But you will learn the three reasons that public opinion polls don't really tell us anything about public opinion.

1. You'll deliver an opinion—whether you've got one or not. Suppose you really don't care what may have gone on behind the closed doors of an elected officer. Maybe you haven't been keeping up with the situation in

Afghanistan, either, or spending much time fretting over our trade imbalance with China. But you don't want to look stupid in front of the man holding the clipboard, pencil poised, waiting for your insightful comment.

So you give an answer.

Whatever answer you give, it may not really be your opinion. More likely, the pollster gets the opinion you gave because you felt you had to give one. This isn't useful information.

2. The question means everything and thus doesn't mean anything. In the context of the example question, what does "immoral activity" really mean? That all depends on who's doing the moralizing. The phrase means different things to different people. Because it can mean *anything*, it really means *nothing*. How can the pollster evaluate your "yes" or "no" response without knowing your definition? Context is key.

Take a look at another part of that question: "who has been caught engaging." Does that mean "caught in the act"? Or does it mean "suspected" or "accused"? Maybe it means "convicted." How you interpret the wording affects how you respond to the question.

3. The question implies that there is a "right" answer. Look at the question again: "Do you feel that a person who has been caught engaging in immoral activity can be trusted to serve in high elected office?"

Notice that you're given a binary, closed choice: your answer should be "yes" or "no." There's no room on the pollster's chart for "maybe" or "that depends on what you mean by 'immoral activity'" or "'caught' in what way?" or even "which high elected office?"

You've got to fit your response into one of two extreme slots.

Your definition of "immoral activity," if you buy into the concept at all, probably carries a negative connotation. "Immoral" is bad. "Caught" is also bad.

On the other hand, "trusted" is good. So the wording of the question and the yes/no choice oversimplify a complex situation. You're asked if you would give something good (trust) to a bad person (someone caught engaging in immoral activity).

You know, then, that the "right" (socially approved) answer—the one the smiling pollster with the clipboard expects from a fine, upstanding citizen like you—is "no."

That doesn't mean you'll *say* "no," of course. You might say "yes" simply to defy social expectation. Either way, you're reacting to the way the question is *worded* and not necessarily its content.

Why Ask Questions?

Asking your staff questions and looking for feedback offers two immediate benefits—regardless of what answers you get.

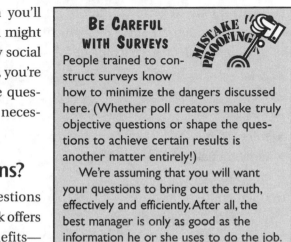

BE CAREFUL WITH SURVEYS

People trained to construct surveys know how to minimize the dangers discussed here. (Whether poll creators make truly objective questions or shape the questions to achieve certain results is another matter entirely!)

We're assuming that you will want your questions to bring out the truth, effectively and efficiently. After all, the best manager is only as good as the information he or she uses to do the job.

When you're listening, you're learning. No matter how useful the answer is in practical terms, it reveals information about the person who gave it. You'll discover a lot about workers' attitudes as well as aptitudes by listening to their responses.

When you're asking, you're expressing respect. Workers may not thank you for asking, but they'll feel good about it. You wouldn't have asked if you didn't want to know. You've brought them into the decision-making process and shown your respect for their knowledge and experience.

You win just by the very act of asking.

AVOID "BLUFF THE BOSS" SMART

MANAGING

Why should you never answer a question with a question? Why not?

If you ask a question they don't understand, you had better hope they ask for clarification. That's a lot better than having them play Bluff the Boss—nodding, smiling, and giving you an answer, any answer, just to get you off their backs and back in your cubicle where you belong. Don't become impatient if your question brings a question in response. It's a good sign that the other person is asking for clarification.

The Qualities of Effective Coaching Questions

It isn't easy to ask a question that doesn't fall into one or more of the traps we just discussed—or any others. You'll need to ask effective questions if you really intend to get useful information from the people who work with you and support them in their growth. That's why you need to learn the qualities of effective coaching questions. Good questions are

- brief
- clear
- focused
- relevant
- constructive
- neutral
- open-ended.

Let's look at each of these qualities.

An effective question is *brief*. So is an effective speech, marriage proposal, or court brief, and for the same basic reasons.

- Your listener's attention span is limited. (That depends a lot on interest and engagement. You probably have a little more latitude for a marriage proposal.)
- Words written on the wind tend to blow away. If your question is long or convoluted, by the time you get to the end, your listener may have forgotten the first part.
- The longer the question, the more likely you are to confuse your listener. Short sentences aren't only easier to understand; they're also easier to say.

TRICKS OF THE TRADE

KEEPING QUESTIONS BRIEF

To keep your question brief, think about it ahead of time. Specifically, consider two things: (1) What do you want to learn from the answer? (2) What words will best elicit this information?

If possible, rehearse your question, honing a key phrase or two. As you do so, visualize yourself delivering the questions just the way you want to.

This system works for any kind of public speaking, by the way, as well as for making more effective inquiries in writing.

An effective question is *clear*. "Do you think we should veto the proposal to discontinue the policy of rejecting parts that haven't successfully gone through the nonmandatory inspection?"

That question is almost good enough to qualify as a referendum in the next election—one of those ballot initiatives that needs an explanation: "Note: A 'no' vote on this proposal indicates your support for continuing to reject parts that haven't passed inspection. A 'yes' vote means you're in favor of changing the current policy."

If you veto a proposal to stop doing whatever it is you're doing now, you would be agreeing to continue doing what you're doing, right? So ask, "Should we keep rejecting parts if they haven't passed inspection?"

Clear questions avoid:

- *Passive voice.* A passive construction like "the offer is to be evaluated" or "the work is to be completed on time" often fails to specify something important—the person or people responsible for the action. Who's going to be evaluating that offer or completing that work?
- *Fog.* Sometimes big words and jargon happen to get in the way of communication. That's fog. (If the confusion is intentional, as part of a smoke screen, it's called *smog.*) For example, what does the phrase "managerial compensatory alternatives" mean? Is it ways to make up for some deficiency? *By* managers or *to* managers? Or is it choices of payment? Again, is the payment *by* managers or *to* managers? If managers make the payment, is the choice up to them or to whoever receives the payment?
- *Multiple negatives.* We don't mean only to avoid asking questions like "Don't nobody here know nothing?" (What your fourth-grade teacher told you about grammar may be right, but it's not enough to ensure good questions.) Consider our question "Do you think we should veto [negative] the proposal to discontinue [negative] the policy of rejecting [negative] parts that haven't [negative] successfully gone through the nonmandatory inspection?" No wonder it defies understanding!

An effective question is *focused*. Target a single subject and a particular aspect of that subject per question. Otherwise you may render any answer meaningless.

Suppose you ask, "Do you think that a simplification in the development process, specifically eliminating the initial discussion, the storyboard, or the focus group, or any two of those steps, would result in a reduction in the quality of the final editorial product, if we also brought in an outside coder to beta-test all programs before release?"

The response is likely to be "Huh?" or "Could you repeat the question?" Even if you get an answer of "yes" or "no," it won't be much more useful, because you won't know what it means—which you'll find out as soon as you echo that answer.

"So you think we ought to get rid of the focus groups?"

"I didn't say that. I like the focus groups."

"Well, then, you want to drop the storyboarding?"

"No, we need the storyboarding. Why would I want to drop it?"

"But you said . . ."

You can imagine how the discussion goes on from here.

Break questions into their component parts, and ask them sequentially.

Q: Do you think we could eliminate the initial discussion without hurting the quality of the program?

A: Sure. Those discussions are a complete waste of time.

Q: How about the storyboard?

A: No way. That's where we figure out how to make the program flow properly.

Q: What do you think of the focus group?

A: It doesn't seem necessary, at least as part of the routine process.

Q: What if we hired a freelance coder to beta-test everything after we're done with it?

A: An outsider wouldn't catch the kind of mistakes I'm talking about.

Q: Can you give me an example?

Now you're getting useful feedback, without the frustration and confusion your multipart question would cause.

An effective question is *relevant*. Have you ever been "blindsided" by an irrelevant question? The surprise question might work for attack journalism and in TV courtroom dramas, but it doesn't do much good in the office. Be clear about your purpose and honest about your motives. Keep your questions on subject and on target. If an answer strays off the point, tactfully refocus.

Suppose you ask, "What if we hired a freelancer to edit our documents after we're done with it?" The response might be, "First we hire a bunch of consultants to tell us how to run the production process, and now you want to bring in an editor to hack up our copy! Why don't we just can the editorial staff and ship the whole thing out?"

The mention of "consultants" sounds an alarm in your head. Maybe you were against hiring them from the start, but you got voted down. This is a perfect chance to vent your spleen and let somebody know that the resulting mess wasn't your fault.

Don't do it. You've got another problem on the table, and there may be no connection between the production consultants and the potential editorial freelancer.

Instead, reply, "I share your concern about consultants, but we need to talk through the editorial process right now. I really need your feedback on this." You will use your coaching skills of being focused to keep the conversation on track.

An effective question is *constructive*. Accentuate the positive in your approach to questioning, not because it makes you seem nicer but because your questions will be more effective. It will open up possibilities for change and growth, rather than looking to point fingers and assign blame. Let's look at the difference between asking a question with a negative slant or wording and asking a similar question in a positive way.

Negative: "How can we get people to stop skipping the meetings?" ["What should we do to punish people who don't come to meetings?"] (Notice how this focuses on "skipping" and punishment.)

Positive: "How can we get people to attend the meetings?" "How can we make the meetings better, so everyone will show up?"

POSITIVE-COMMAND BRAIN

Did you know that the human brain is a positive-command system? This means that the brain filters out negatives like "don't" or "not." Imagine if I said to you, "Quick! *Do not* think about a red bouncing rubber ball!" Of course, you immediately see a red ball **TOOLS** boinging across your mental image. That's because your brain doesn't hear the *not* in that command, it only hears and processes the rest. If you ask a question in a negative way, the person will focus on the negative things in the sentence. If you want to open up possibilities for change, word the question or statement so that you highlight what you *do want*.

AVOID EUPHEMISMS

Be careful when you're taking a positive approach to pose a constructive question that you don't slip into euphemistic phrasings.

Negative: "How can we get people to stop skipping the meetings?"

Euphemistic rephrasing (still negative): "What negative sanctions and disincentives can we employ to ensure full attendance at meetings?"

The second question still leads to a discussion of punishments. The only difference is that you'll be using bigger words—and a lot more time—to get there.

Whatever you ask, ask it clearly and simply.

It's more than just a matter of phrasing. You're asking two different questions, and you'll get two different answers.

Admittedly, discussing the negative question could be a lot more fun, but discussing the positive question will be much more productive, leading to genuine improvements—which may even mean eliminating an unnecessary meeting.

Sometimes, even when you ask a positive question, the person will have a negative response. You could ask, "How could we improve communications between the sales department and the public relations department?" Imagine the person replies, "I don't know, but what we have now just isn't working! PR doesn't respond to e-mails, and Sales never seems to have any good suggestions!"

Some people go straight to the negative and need a little prodding to think about the positive. You can follow up with, "Okay, so if e-mail isn't working, what *would* work?" Stay persistent on getting to a solution.

An effective question is *neutral*. Don't confuse "neutral" with "neutered." A good question may be controversial. (The most interesting ones are.) But it doesn't imply the "right" answer through biased wording.

Here's an example of the same question, first asked in a way that implies a "yes" answer, then with a built-in "no" response, and finally phrased in a "value-neutral" manner.

Implied "yes" question: "Do you think we should improve overall quality by hiring a freelance editor?" (Who wouldn't be in favor of improving overall quality?)

Implied "no" question: "Do you think we should add an extra step to the editorial process by hiring a freelance editor?" (Who would favor adding an extra step?)

Value-neutral question: "What do you think about hiring a freelance editor?" (Elicits more opinions than just "yes" or "no.")

An effective question is *open-ended*. Ask a "yes" or "no" question, and you'll get (at best) a "yes" or "no" answer. That's all. So often, that's not enough.

Consider this scenario. You've got a bottleneck in the production process. You're not sure how to unsnarl things, so you do the smart thing and ask the folks on the front line.

Q: Should we hire another online supervisor?

A: No way!

End of discussion. If you want more, you'll have to go fishing.

Q: How come?

A: It's a bad idea.

Q: Do you think it would be a waste of money?

A: You bet.

Q: So, you don't think there'd be any advantage to the hire?

A: Nope.

This isn't a discussion. It's like pulling impacted wisdom teeth. You're no closer to an answer, or even a useful suggestion, than when you started.

If you want to know whether the folks on the line think they need another supervisor, you asked the right question—and you got a clear answer. But if you want to explore possible solutions to a production problem, ask an open-ended question: "What can we do to fix the problem on the line?"

This new question, though admirably open-ended, fails the "value-neutral" test, as it clearly emphasizes that there is a problem. Instead of useful answers, you will more likely get defensive attitudes. Rephrase your question one more time: "What can we do to speed up production on the line?"

This question doesn't point the finger and say that production is "too slow" (a problem for which somebody must be at fault). It just says you'd like to explore ways to speed things up.

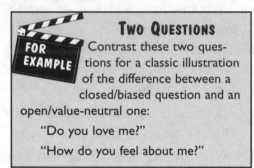

TWO QUESTIONS
Contrast these two questions for a classic illustration of the difference between a closed/biased question and an open/value-neutral one:

"Do you love me?"

"How do you feel about me?"

It takes a bit of thought to ask a value-neutral and open-ended question. Make sure you give each question your careful attention.

By the way, an effective manager might frame the question with a positive comment about production. If you begin, for example, with "We've all been very pleased with the teamwork shown on the production line and the quality of our products," you can more easily and safely ask the question "Now, what can we do to speed up production on the line?"

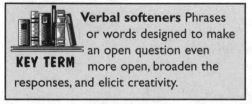

Verbal softeners Phrases or words designed to make an open question even more open, broaden the responses, and elicit creativity.

To get a truly open-ended question and start a conversation that brings forth a lot of possibilities, you may need to employ *verbal softeners*, which are phrases and words you can use to broaden the scope of a question. When you use them, you can open up new possibilities and creativity from your employee. You take the pressure off being "right" or having a "good answer."

For example, let's take the question "What should we do to speed up production?" As we've established, this is a positive, value-neutral question that is open-ended. By using verbal softeners here, you create more opportunities for the respondent to think creatively.

- "What *can* [or *could*] we do to speed up production?" (Note that "should" in the original question implies that a recommendation must be given, and the employee may not be comfortable with this yet. "Can" and "could" look at possibilities.)
- "What are *some of the ways* we could speed up production?" (Start brainstorming before asking for a decision or recommendation.)
- "How *might we start* to speed up production?" (Baby steps. No need to come up with a complete solution, although one may come forth in the conversation.)

Verbal softeners can help elicit the other person's resourcefulness and creativity as you sort through possibilities and options together.

Seven Major Types of Questions

There are seven main categories of questions: factual, explanatory, justifying, leading, hypothetical, alternative, and summary. Let's take a look at when to use them and when to avoid them.

1. Factual Questions. The question "How many online supervisors do we employ?" asks for a number, not an evaluation. It's a question that seeks a factual answer.

"How many online supervisors do we need?" asks for a number, but it's not a factual question. To answer that, you must give an opinion.

"Is it raining?" is a factual question. "How's the weather?" isn't factual, although it might evoke the same information: "It's raining!" It could also involve an opinion: "It's great!" (from a farmer) or "Lousy!" (from a landscaper who can't work) for the same light, misty rain.

You can verify the answer to a factual question by checking a second or third source. For the first question, count the number of online supervisors on the payroll (assuming they all actually carry the same job title, of course). For the second question, stick your head outside and see if you get wet. You can't "verify" an opinion question.

If you want facts, ask factual questions. You may find it useful to begin

DON'T ARGUE ABOUT OPINIONS

You'll waste a lot of time if you argue about the responses to an opinion question as if it were a factual question. Because you can't verify an opinion, you can't prove it to be correct or incorrect. I can prove to you that it's raining, but I can't prove that the rain constitutes "great" or "lousy" weather, as that's a matter of perspective.

coaching sessions with factual questions to establish common understanding and background.

2. Explanatory Questions. Most kids go through a "why?" stage. Parents of kids in this stage often find themselves running out of answers and patience: "Why do I have to take a nap now?" "Why do I have to eat my green beans?" "Why does Mommy wear red stuff on her lips?" "Why is it raining?"

"Why?" is a basic explanatory question. It can make a fine follow-up question.

"What can we do to speed things up on line?"

"Get rid of that new supervisor!"

"Why?"

Be careful how you ask "Why?" Your tone of voice can make all the difference between a "Why?" that means "What makes you think so?" and a "Why?" that means "You stupid idiot." Inject some genuine curiosity into asking "why?"

Ask without conveying any other meaning with tone of voice, gestures, or facial expression (which can often turn your "why?" into "why not?"). If you can, asking "why?" will serve you well.

3. Justifying Questions. That versatile little word *why* can also signal a justifying question.

You may have heard this key question on almost any reality TV show that involves a competition (*Top Chef*, *Project Runway*, or *Hell's Kitchen*, for example). At some point, the judges ask a contestant who might be up for elimination: "Why should you stay in this competition?" The response usually is a pouring forth of justifications and promises to succeed.

Asking "Why?" in response to the suggestion to get rid of the online supervisor can mean "Why should we get rid of the online supervisor?" (explanatory) or "Why do you think so?" (justifying). If you intended to ask the first question but got an answer to the second, everybody walks away confused. Ask for what you want.

Most often, you will want explanation rather than justification. It's difficult to ask for justification without putting someone on the defensive. Too often, justifying questions sound like "Says who?" For that reason, it's best to avoid this category.

A simple phrase change might help you get a more informative response and avoid justification. Instead of asking "why?," try to ask "how?" In the example of asking about the new online supervisor, instead of asking why you should get rid of him, ask "How would that help?"

4. Leading Questions. As the name suggests, this type of question leads the responder toward a desired answer. Phone solicitors use this tactic all the time.

At its worst (and phone solicitation is surely an example of the worst), the leading probe serves as a rhetorical question, which is asked to make a point or elicit a set response rather than to gather information. At its best, this type of question is still pretty annoying. Avoid asking leading questions.

Common examples of leading questions include ones that start with "Don't you think . . . ?" or "Don't you *want* to do XYZ?" In the case of whether to dismiss the line supervisor, a leading question might be "Don't you think that would hurt productivity?" You can obviously see how the speaker's own opinion is worded in this phrasing. The employee immediately gets the picture that you think firing the supervisor is a bad idea, and that you aren't necessarily open to suggestion. He will hush up and agree with you rather than make waves.

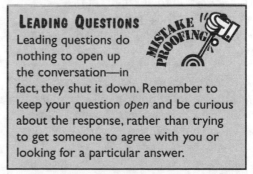

LEADING QUESTIONS

Leading questions do nothing to open up the conversation—in fact, they shut it down. Remember to keep your question *open* and be curious about the response, rather than trying to get someone to agree with you or looking for a particular answer.

5. Hypothetical Questions. These are your basic "what if?" questions. At their best and most useful, they call for creative thinking based on knowledge, an estimate, or educated guess. At their worst, they call for speculation, a "wild guess." If you follow up this wild speculation

> **Manipulate** To manage or control in an unfair or fraudulent way. This one
> **KEY TERM** comes with a warning: Don't do it. Not even once. Not by what you do, or what you say, or how you say it. Your staff won't trust you again—and they'll be right not to.

with a little dose of reality, you can elicit some truly creative responses to issues at hand.

In either case, a hypothetical question asks someone to comment on circumstances that haven't happened (and might never happen).

Suppose you ask a shift supervisor, "How much of a drop-off in production do you think we would experience if we eliminated two workers from each shift?" The shift supervisor should be in a position to give you at least an educated guess, based on past productivity and his or her knowledge of work flow. The same question, asked of one of the shift workers, probably calls for some broader speculation.

When you ask this question of a supervisor who has already stated strong opposition to reducing the workforce, it becomes *manipulative*, more of a weapon than a sincere attempt to gather information.

"Okay," you say, "I understand that you don't want to lay anybody off. Neither do I. But just suppose we did reduce the force by two workers per shift. How do you think that would affect productivity?"

The supervisor grudgingly dredges up a number—which you then use to justify the layoffs. The supervisor probably feels manipulated—and will be wary of answering another question from you.

> **"JUST SUPPOSE ..."**
> In the example in the text, saying "just suppose" led to a grudging response. However,
> **TOOLS** this phrase can be a powerful way to visualize new opportunities. You can ask your employees "Just suppose we were able to increase productivity in some way. How might that affect you? The department? The whole company?" Questions like these help employees connect immediate goals and tasks with the bigger picture, which can then fuel motivation.

6. Alternative Questions. When asking these kinds of questions, you provide the alternative responses, essentially like a multiple-choice test. Evaluation forms provide a classic example: "Write the number that best corresponds with your reaction: 5, agree strongly; 4, agree; 3, neither agree nor disagree; 2, disagree; 1, disagree strongly." These kinds of questions can be helpful when quantifying a qualitative response, but can also be limiting because people don't always fit neatly in boxes.

Preference and personality tests pose an either/or choice:

- "Would you rather be (a) a sanitation engineer or (b) a forest ranger?"
- "Would you rather be (a) a professional athlete or (b) a college professor?"
- "Would you rather be (a) Dr. Oz or (b) Dr. Phil?"

By suggesting choices, you make it easier to respond. But you also limit that response. Your respondent might not want to be either a sanitation engineer or a forest ranger, but you've forced a choice.

A forced choice may also be manipulative. Instead of asking for a general assessment of potential layoffs on productivity, suppose you ask, "Should we lay off one, two, or three operators per shift?" The answer "None" isn't an option.

7. Summary Questions. As governor of California and then as president, Ronald Reagan required staffers to prepare mini-memos on important issues. From air pollution to the Strategic Defense Initiative, Reagan wanted their best judgment rendered in one crisp paragraph.

Supporters called him the Great Communicator. Detractors dubbed him the Great Simplifier. Either way, he required that his advisers be great synthesizers.

When you ask a summary question, you're saying, "I don't have time to do the math; I just want the bottom line. I have no patience for close-ups; I want the big picture." You put blinders on to context, reasoning, and other information that might be very important.

Summary questions often begin with phrases like "In general" and "Overall" and can be a productive category of questions for you as a manager. Keep in mind, though, that summary questions are often hard to answer and may come across as threatening. Having to come up with an overall assessment can take time, thought, and even in-depth research.

Three Techniques for Asking Questions

Here are three techniques on how to ask appropriate questions and ensure better responses.

1. Give employees time to think. Silence is an acceptable answer and a valuable tool. So is the statement "I don't know." If the question requires thought, provide time and opportunity for thought to take place. Avoid handing out new material at a meeting, for example, and then asking for an immediate response. You might get a gut-reaction response (which can be useful, if that's what you are looking for), but if you want a well-thought-out answer, wait a bit.

2. Tell employees what's at stake. Most of us learn to associate questions with tests and grades. The teacher knows the answers; she wants to see if *you* know them. You can be right or wrong; when you're wrong, if you're lucky, you might get partial credit.

What do employees win or lose when they answer your question? Will they be punished for a "wrong" answer, an answer you don't want to hear? If so, you'll probably never get an honest answer.

How binding are their answers? Can they change their minds later? Will their answers factor into your decision? Or are you just asking to be asking and tend to ignore their input?

Be honest about your motives for asking and what you intend to do with the responses. In most cases, you're asking for advice, not taking a vote. You aren't bound to act according to the advice you receive. But the input should make a difference or else you shouldn't ask.

If your actions contradict the information you get, explain why.

If you ask the question simply to give the impression of wanting an answer (without any real intention to do so), you'll do more damage to your working relationships than if you never asked at all.

3. When you're done asking, shut up and listen. We look at ways to become a more effective listener in the next chapter.

The Coach's Checklist for Chapter 5

☑ Effective questions help you get useful information from the people who work with you. They also help people get at what they might not realize they know, and they help everyone become aware of what they need to do to improve.

☑ Good coaching questions that will help people learn and improve are *brief, clear, focused, relevant, constructive, neutral,* and *open-ended.*

☑ There are seven main categories of questions: *factual, explanatory, justifying, leading, hypothetical, alternative,* and *summary.*

☑ Here are three ways for getting better responses to your questions: (1) give employees time to think about their responses; (2) tell them what's at stake, why you need this information; and (3) when you're done asking, be quiet and listen.

Powerful Listening

We all spend a lot of time in school learning how to communicate. We take classes in written communication and many take courses in technical writing, business writing, speech, or debate. We learn how to express ourselves.

But who learns how to *listen*?

It's a crucial skill for any manager, especially if you manage by coaching.

Three Levels of Listening

You've almost certainly heard of *active listening*, which requires attentive listening and careful processing of what is heard. This technique can certainly help you build better relationships, but you'll need to go deeper to create an effective coaching relationship.

You may have also heard of *nonviolent communication*, developed by Marshall Rosenberg, which is a process for people to communicate with compassion and clarity. It's focused around honest self-expression and empathy.

Elements of active listening and nonviolent communication come into play when you're coaching your employees. Good coaches know that powerful listening helps you hear more than is being said, leaves you open to intuition, and allows you to help the other person connect to a bigger picture. To do this consistently and effectively, you need to know the three levels of listening.

Level 1 Listening

Most people live "in their heads" every day. We are constantly thinking about what we are doing, what's coming up next, getting distracted by things around us. We have an almost nonstop internal dialogue. We are aware of our surroundings and other people in terms of how they affect us.

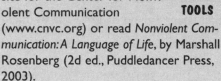

Active listening The act of attentively and consciously listening to another, to hear more than just the **KEY TERMS** words being said. These skills are important for coaching.

Nonviolent communication Centers around honest self-expression, compassion, and empathy between communicators. It leads to greater authenticity and deeper understanding.

NONVIOLENT COMMUNICATION

To learn more, visit the Web site for the Center for Nonviolent Communication **TOOLS** (www.cnvc.org) or read *Nonviolent Communication: A Language of Life*, by Marshall Rosenberg (2d ed., Puddledancer Press, 2003).

Thus, in conversation, we practice *level 1 listening*, also called "head-centered listening." In this kind of listening, we tend to hear and absorb about a fourth to half of what the other person is saying. We look for ways to respond from our own viewpoint, like a conversational tennis match. Each statement you lob at me, I come back with a similar response, back and forth. There's some connection here, but it's superficial.

To use the analogy of a football game, level 1 listening takes place on the field, between players—what is immediately affecting us, right here, right now.

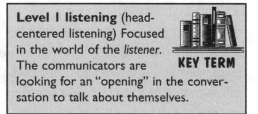

Level I listening (head-centered listening) Focused in the world of the *listener*. The communicators are **KEY TERM** looking for an "opening" in the conversation to talk about themselves.

At a social party, level 1 listening might go like this.

Dan: So, Sandy, do you have any kids?

Sandy: I have two boys.

Dan: That's nice! I have a boy and two girls myself.

Sandy: What ages?

Dan: The girls are twins, 11 years old, and my son is just four.

Sandy: My oldest son is 12 and my baby is seven.

Dan: What school do they go to?

Sandy: Fairbanks Elementary. They like the sports program a lot.

Dan: My daughters go to the Ravencroft Academy. My wife and I felt the technology advantage was worth the tuition cost.

Sandy: We do a lot of educational stuff on the weekends—go to museums and the zoo.

Dan: That's always fun. We like to take it easy after a long week, ourselves!

As you can see from this dialogue, Dan and Sandy seem to be looking for opportunities to talk about themselves and express their own opinions. In fact, Dan seems to be subtly bragging about sending his daughters to a private school, which makes Sandy feel a bit defensive about the public school her kids go to, so she responds with the comment about educational outings. Dan's rejoinder about relaxing on the weekend might be a subtle dig at Sandy's choices. Although Dan and Sandy seem to be getting to know each other, the details here are fairly superficial.

Level 1 listening is what you will experience in the workplace a lot—it's a natural state, our default mode. It takes effort and awareness to move into the next levels of listening, which can lift your interactions into the realms of deeper meaning and more possibilities.

Level 2 Listening

The next stage beyond level 1 listening is *level 2 listening*, also called "heart-centered listening." Don't let the word *heart* fool you—it's not necessarily about loving the other person! In level 2 listening, you consciously slide out of your own worldview (move from your head to an open heart) so that you can learn more about the speaker. You ask a lot of questions instead of looking for a conversational opening to interject your own point of view. You "get amnesia" about your own life for a while so that you can really learn about and connect with the other person.

> **Level 2 listening** (heart-centered listening) Focused in the world of the *speaker*. The listener asks questions **KEY TERM** to learn more about the other person, without looking for a way to talk about him- or herself.

In level 2 listening, you will use active listening skills as well as some of the principles of nonviolent communication. You focus attentively on the other person. You keep asking questions or inviting more comments. This opens the door for a deeper connection and more relevant information to come out.

To return to the analogy of a football game, level 2 listening takes place in the stands, perhaps about halfway up. The speaker might still be on the field, but the listener is looking to see how that "player" is moving around and how the game is progressing as a whole.

Ever heard the saying, "If you want to be *interesting*, be *interested*"? That's how level 2 listening works. People will find you fascinating if you simply ask *them* a lot of questions (even if you don't say a word about yourself). They feel heard, listened to, and valued. You don't express any judgment or analysis (much less any advice) in this kind of listening (although you may think about it!). You are simply focused on the other person. When was the last time *you* were listened to like that? Try it with family members or at a party—see how people react to being listened to this way.

Here's how Dan and Sandy's conversation might go if Dan was practicing level 2 listening.

Dan: So, Sandy, do you have any kids?

Sandy: I have two boys.

Dan: What ages?

Sandy: My oldest son is 12 and my baby is seven.

Dan: What school do they go to?

Sandy: Fairbanks Elementary. They like the sports program a lot.

Dan: What sports do they play?

Sandy: They really like soccer, and in the summer they do a lot of swimming.

Dan: What do you like to do when they are kicking the ball around?

Sandy: Well, I'm actually an assistant coach on Danny's team, and we like to play a little family soccer on the weekend, if we're not going to a museum or the zoo!

In this conversation, Dan has asked follow-up questions, rather than volunteering his own information and viewpoint. He's learned a lot more about Sandy and her kids. From Sandy's last statement, he can probably deduce that she likes to be active in her sons' lives and they like to do things together as a family. Her values start to show up in the conversation, and she probably feels a deeper connection to Dan because she has shared some of the things that are important to her.

SMART MANAGING

QUESTIONING AND LISTENING

We talked about asking questions with genuine curiosity in Chapter 5. Pair this with level 2 listening and you have an extremely effective tool for tapping into the potential of your employees. Ask the question, then turn on your level 2 listening, and see what your team members come up with. This kind of listening demonstrates how much you value their input, increasing their engagement.

Level 3 Listening

An even higher level of communication is known as *level 3 listening*, or "coach position." This level of listening not only focuses on the world of the speaker, it also connects with the bigger picture of the world (or business)—you're listening *globally*. When coaching as a manager, you can use level 3 listening to first connect with your employee's thoughts and opinions, elicit their creativity, and then connect their thoughts with the department's, company's, and industry's larger goals or purpose.

This kind of bigger thinking (or "listening with bigger ears" as it's sometimes called) not only offers all the respect and value that comes with level 2 listening, it then encourages the speaker to think even bigger, connecting his or her viewpoint and thoughts to a broader vision. There is no judgment, analysis, or advice in pure level 3 listening, and the coach is unattached to the outcome. In coach position, you step into the person's model of the world, stay centered on him or her, yet have the capacity to bring in more viewpoints as appropriate.

> **Level 3 listening** (coach position) Focused on the speaker as connected to a bigger picture. This kind of listening helps the speaker feel valued and connects his or her communication to a larger picture.

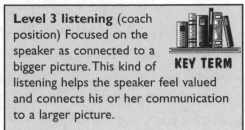

KEY TERM

To return to the football game analogy one more time, level 3 listening takes place in the skybox, where the listener can see the whole game and the stands. From this height, you can invite the "player" up to the skybox with you to get an overview. (You can go further, all the way up to the "blimp view" sometimes!)

A good coach holds a very clean coach position, which allows the client to begin in her own world, tap her potential, and then shift higher to think how her actions might make bigger ripples in her own life and the world at large.

LEVELS 2 AND 3 LISTENING

TRICKS OF THE TRADE

You may find it difficult to leap straight from being a manager into level 3 listening. Move into level 2 first, so you can be truly present and focused and create rapport. As the coaching conversation moves toward solutions, bring in level 3 listening, where you can help the employee see the ripple effects of his actions.

A visual that might help you step into the coach position is that of climbing a snowy mountain peak. At the top, you see a lot more of the world, and your own issues become insignificant in the majesty of the scenery surrounding you. Your employee may still be climbing the mountain, and your job is to reach a hand down and lift him so he can join you at the top.

Let's return to Dan and Sandy's conversation. Dan began in level 2 listening before, and found out that Sandy likes to coach her son's soccer team and have educational outings with her family on the weekend. Now he moves into a level 3 approach, asking questions that help him find out more about her values and life.

Dan: Wow, sports, museums, and zoos! Sounds like you are really busy!

Sandy: I am, but I love it. I work flex time as a paralegal so I can have the time to spend with my family. They are my main priority, but I like the work I do, too. I'm glad I didn't have to give it up entirely.

Dan: (*grinning*) Do you ever get a vacation?

Sandy: Oh sure! We go camping a lot in the spring and take a big trip in the fall. We're an adventurous bunch, and we like to see the world!

Dan: What was your favorite trip so far?

Sandy: (*laughs*) It seems silly to say, but I just loved going to Disney World! I hadn't been since I was young, and it was just wonderful to see the boys' faces light up. Plus, it brought back some great memories of my family going together and me fighting with my sister over the e-tickets.

Dan: If you could go anywhere on vacation, where would you go?

Sandy: There's so much I want to see that it's hard to choose! If money and time were no object, I think I'd love to go on a long tour of Japan. I've always been fascinated with the culture and their history.

Dan has learned a lot more about Sandy in this exchange! He can tell that she likes her work, but her family is her top priority. She likes to camp and travel, so she clearly values adventurous experiences (she even says so quite clearly). He might also infer that she likes to learn new things, as she mentioned being fascinated with a foreign culture and wanting to really experience it. From this conversation, Dan gets a much bigger view of Sandy's values and life goals.

In a business setting, your coaching conversations will be a lot more focused on a particular topic. (See Chapter 7 for clear directions on solution-focused coaching.) You can bring in level 3 listening by asking the following kinds of questions in a session.

- What results might that plan have?
- How might the department (company, industry) be affected?
- What might change around you when this is implemented?
- If you accomplish this, what are the effects on your career?
- How does this plan (or anticipated results) factor into your goals for the year?

Now that you have a strong overview of the levels of listening and how they help you be a better coach, let's delve into some other aspects of listening.

Seven Keys to Effective Listening

Let's explore seven basic techniques to help you be a better listener.

1. Be prepared. A good news reporter does background research before interviewing a source. Reporters need basic information to be able to ask the right questions and understand the answers.

The same goes for a workplace coach. You wouldn't go into a meeting without an agenda, and meetings run best and most efficiently when people are *prepared*.

Look over the personnel file, scan the quarterly report, brush up on key terms you don't use every day, review any relevant e-mails or notes you have about the issue at hand. Anticipate responses and follow-up questions. As little as two or three minutes of preparation can make the difference between a useful coaching session and a mutual waste of time. Use the time to become focused and centered, so you can easily step into level 2 and then level 3 listening.

2. Drop everything. The biggest compliment you can pay another human being is giving your full, undivided attention. Effective listening requires nothing less.

For example, don't shuffle through a stack of papers, don't examine the pattern of holes in the ceiling panels or the scene out the window, and most important, don't keep working.

Time management systems teach us how to do two, three, even four things at once. That's great—when you're dealing with tasks.

For interacting with people, you should concentrate on doing one thing at a time—and doing it well. Any second activity is a distraction that risks undermining your communication—and it's likely to bother or even offend the other person. Your computer won't care if you're reading mail and checking your phone

DO NOT DISTURB

TRICKS OF THE TRADE

One wise manager had a very effective habit. As soon as somebody entered her office, she would immediately reach over and press the "Do Not Disturb" button on her phone.

That move had two important effects. It kept the phone from ringing, of course. But it was also a clear sign of respect, offering quiet assurance that the visitor was important.

messages while running a program. But people are different. So when you listen, just listen.

Two specific interruptions (phone calls and clock watching) are so intrusive that they deserve further discussion.

One of the most irritating dramas in modern daily life begins when the phone rings. When you leap to answer it, you abandon the person who took the trouble to meet with you face to face. You're telling that person that somebody else is more important than he or she is.

Transfer your calls so the phone doesn't even chirp. Or let your voice mail work its magic. Silence your cell phone so you aren't alerted to every call, text message, e-mail, or voice mail.

As with the telephone, so, too, with the clock watching.

We're not suggesting you lose track of time. A clearly defined time limit is one of the hallmarks of an effective coaching session. Just stop looking at your watch or the clock when you're supposed to be listening.

If you don't think you look at that watch a lot, take it off for a day, and see how many times you catch yourself glancing at your wrist. You'll discover how watch-dependent you really are. You'll also discover that in our society, it's just about impossible not to know what time it is, even without a watch. Time reminders are everywhere.

TRICKS OF THE TRADE

AN UNOBTRUSIVE TIMER

Most businesspeople carry smart phones these days. Almost all smart phones have some sort of alarm, timer, or countdown application. To respect any time limit you have on meeting with someone, set your alarm beforehand to alert you when, say, five minutes are left. Let the person know that you are setting the alarm only so that you can both respect each other's time. Choose an alarm sound that's soothing and calming, rather than loud and abrupt. A chime such as harp strings or running water will be a gentle alert to wrap things up.

Here are just three ways to keep track of time:

- Sit where you can see a wall or desk clock without having to turn your head. (It's a plus if you can check the time without shifting your eyes.)
- Set your computer or cell phone to cue you five minutes before you need to wrap up (see sidebar tip above on An Unobtrusive Timer).

- If you have to look at a watch, do it while you're talking, not when you're listening. (That way you also might become more aware of how much you're talking, and you may listen more.)

3. Maintain eye contact. If you're not peeking at your watch or staring out the window, what are you looking at?

Try looking at the person you're talking with. Direct eye contact establishes a powerful connection and demonstrates your focus.

Lack of eye contact is one of the reasons phone conversations are more likely to create misunderstandings—even though you have tone of voice, inflection, and immediate feedback to help you. People reveal much about their feelings and comprehension through their eyes.

If you find it difficult to look someone in the eye, you probably aren't used to doing it. Take a deep breath and take a peek. Or focus on the bridge of the person's nose, between the eyes.

DON'T LEAD THE WITNESS

SMART

MANAGING

We're all human. We can't always control the impulse to "help out" in a conversation. When you're tempted to grab the words off somebody's tongue or finish their sentence for them, borrow a technique from lawyers: Redirect the conversation.

In court, a leading question often brings an objection from the opposing attorney. In the office, you want to be careful not to lead unnecessarily or ineffectively (see Chapter 5 for more powerful questions). But a skillfully worded and well-timed probe can save you a lot of time and frustration.

As always, tone of voice can be crucial. "Where are we going with this?" can be a gentle prod or an insulting putdown, depending on your tone—and the employee. The best probes are specific, drawing on what your employee has just said:

"Getting back to that point you made about off-site supervision . . ."

"What exactly was the problem with yesterday's output?"

But don't stare. It isn't natural to maintain eye contact for more than a few seconds. Glance away and come back. Reestablish eye contact when you want to stress what you're saying or show you're particularly attentive to what you're hearing. Be aware of your facial expression, too. A hard stare with a firm, tight mouth and frown might indicate disapproval. An open expression, lifted eyebrows, relaxed face, eye contact, and maybe even a tiny smile indicates your openness to the conversation and invites the person to communicate.

4. Hear it all before you respond. "I know what you're going to say."

No, you don't. Saying that you do can be annoying or even insulting. It also destroys effective listening.

In your anxiety to give effective feedback—or maybe to gain control of the conversation, to speed things up a little, or even to save the other person a little effort—you may jump into a statement or question before it's finished (a hallmark of level 1 listening). The result is sometimes comical, sometimes disastrous, but never helpful to communication.

PUT DOWN YOUR PEN

That little pen and the simple notepad can cause trouble. We offer the following advice:

Don't play with the pen and paper. It might not be distracting to move the pad around a little as you listen, but don't flip the pages or tap your pen on the desk or the pad.

Don't doodle. It's a natural impulse for most people, but usually it's the graphic equivalent of twiddling your thumbs. It could suggest that you're bored or thinking of something else.

Don't let any note taking distract the other person. Everybody is curious about what other people are thinking, and those notes are a key to what's going through your mind. Reduce the temptation by keeping your notes close to you, perhaps even resting your hand on them when you're not writing.

Don't anticipate the end of a sentence. Don't assume you know how the statement ends, how the person feels, or where the conversation is leading.

Even if you're really good at guessing what the other person is going to say, fight that urge. Even if your intuition is right, you're wrong for jumping in.

Be patient. Keep your focus. Resist the temptation to intrude. Above all, try not to start framing answers to the next three questions you expect to get.

What if you listen to everything the employee has to say, but you still don't understand?

If you're a smart coach, you take the initiative to get clarity. Your goal is to facilitate effective communication, so it doesn't matter whether the employee didn't say it well or you didn't listen well. Assume the responsibility for getting it right.

Be tactful wording your statements for clarity. "I want to be sure I've got this right." "Just to make sure we're on the same page, here's what I heard." These are judgment-free statements you can use to get clarification.

5. Take notes. You walk a fine line here. You want to keep the discussion informal—coaching is a conversation, not an inquisition. However, taking some brief notes here and there can help you remember to return to key issues, remind yourself of your own action steps, and give you the opportunity to get random thoughts on paper so you can save your attention for the speaker.

There are several advantages to taking notes, besides the obvious purpose of providing a record of the conversation. Here are two benefits for you:

- It keeps you focused. Just try taking notes without listening.
- It keeps you active. As long as your hand is moving, you're not dozing.

Taking notes also provides benefits for the employee. It demonstrates three things:

DON'T WRITE IT ALL DOWN

Don't try to write *everything* down. Complete sentences are unnecessary. Just jot down key words, phrases, and numbers. Leave lots of space around your jottings.

Much of what you write may be useful only during the rest of the session. But you might need to use those notes later to follow up on something or keep a record of the conversation. Go over the notes as soon as possible after the session, filling in the blanks. (That's why it's important to leave a lot of space.) You'll be amazed by how much you remember.

- The topic matters to you.
- The speaker matters to you.
- You're committed to getting the information right.

If you're relaxed about taking notes, you'll be a better listener, and you'll set the other person at ease.

Learn how to take quick notes without breaking your focus on the other person, scribbling quickly while keeping eye contact. Let the employee know that you are taking notes so that you can keep up with the conversation most appropriately.

SMART

MANAGING

NOTES FOR ACTION

Note taking can be a real benefit in some coaching conversations. Encourage your employees to come to you with a notepad or some way of capturing information. That way, they can be sure they remember their own action items and commitments. On the other hand, be willing to share your notes with the employee if asked. Some people (particularly those who might have attention deficit difficulties) find it easier to focus on the big-picture issues of a coaching session if they don't have to take notes themselves, which can be distracting. Sharing your notes with these people helps remind them of what was discussed and agreed on.

6. Acknowledge feelings. People differ vastly in the kinds and amount of emotion they allow themselves to express in the workplace. Many would like to avoid feelings entirely. (We don't discuss the unhealthy effects of that tradition here.) But your conversation with a worker may well go beyond fact or opinion and into feelings. Frustration can lead people to "boil over" and personal feelings *do* come into play in the workplace, no matter how much someone might want to avoid this.

When that happens, don't ignore the feelings as expressed by the other person. Acknowledge and verify them:

- "You sound angry. Tell me about it." (Acknowledges their feelings, invites more explanation)
- "You seem pretty upset. What else is going on here?" (Notices the feelings, seeks a response that might be more comprehensive)
- "I get that you're frustrated about this process. That's natural—anyone in your situation would feel that way." (Validates without belittling or agreeing)

Our previous point about not assuming becomes especially important when feelings are involved. People carry around emotional baggage, pieces of their lives that can spill out unexpectedly. Don't assume you know what may be happening outside the workplace.

By asking, you acknowledge that the employee's feelings are important to you and validate that they are natural. You also avoid trying to deal with feelings that you only perceive, a danger that emerges in the following exchange:

> ### EMOTIONAL BURDEN
> Notice that we talk about acknowledging and verifying (even validating) the other person's feelings. This doesn't necessarily mean you should agree or sympathize. If you express your own sympathizing opinion when coaching, you might just get right down in the muck with your employee, taking on his or her emotional burden. Stepping into that negative energy (fear, anger, frustration) won't help you be a better coach, and it will drain you of your positive energy. Remember to rise to level 3 listening where you can hear and acknowledge, but not take on the emotional burden.

"So, why are you angry?"

"Me? I'm not angry? Why do you assume I'm angry?"

"Well, I don't know. The way you stomped in here, the way you flopped down into the chair, the way you're fidgeting . . . "

"Well, I wasn't angry when I came in here—but I'm sure starting to get irritated!"

7. Allow silence. But don't use it as a weapon. Silence between two human beings—especially in a tense situation—can seem intimidating. Reporters use it as a technique to get a reluctant source to say more than he or she intends.

But a pause that allows for reflection shows respect and allows the employee to give a response that's accurate, rather than just fast.

So now you know about the seven keys to effective listening. You work at following those guidelines. But how can you know if you're becoming a good listener?

To make sure you've understood what you think you've heard, use the following simple system.

1. Receive. To understand it, you have to hear it. Prepare. Be still. Wait. Don't assume. Take notes. Probe gently and redirect the conversation if necessary. Concentrate on the speaker to maintain your focus. Practice the art of doing one thing well.

2. Reflect. Think about what you're hearing. Make sense out of it. Put it into a meaningful context. Ask questions to clarify. Listening is an active process.

SMART

MANAGING

GET THE TRUE ANSWER

Because silence can be unsettling, some will rush to fill the void, rather than using it to think. If you feel that you've gotten a rushed, even inaccurate reply to a question, wait a moment. Even if the other person starts running off at the mouth, sometimes the real answer will come forward if you give him or her enough space.

You can ask the question again if you need to, but be careful how you do so. "Are you sure?" may sound like a challenge. You might try repeating the answer, word for word if necessary. (Sometimes when we hear somebody else echo our words, we think about them differently.) Or you might continue the conversation, asking other questions that return to probe the point, but in different words.

3. Rephrase. "Reflect" also means to bounce light or an image back to the source. That's the next step. Bounce what you're hearing back to the source; then rephrase to make sure you're getting it right.

Do so thoughtfully, using as many words as the other person used to confirm that you respect his or her view of the issue. Avoid psycho-speak, formulaic nonsense like "I hear you saying ..." It can be annoying and can make you focus more on the structure and less on the substance.

Don't be an echo. Begin to put statements and questions into your own words, but check to make sure you have it right so you aren't moving forward on inaccurate assumptions.

Be open to the possibility that you've gotten it wrong. That happens: Nobody's perfect. Don't get defensive. Your job here is to understand.

Moving Beyond Listening

Effective listening is simply a means to an end. Once you have heard and understood, you must *respond*.

That doesn't mean you should take every suggestion, act on every criticism, or effect changes when they're suggested. What it does mean is that you must offer something in return. Often when you respond, you'll take off your coach hat and put on your manager hat. This is entirely appropriate in the workplace. In fact, you might even say directly to an employee, "I have to respond *as a manager* now." Let them know when your role has shifted, and they can shift along with you.

As a manager, you have the right to express your views, but know *when* to do so, so as not to negate any coaching you've done. Do it in the spirit of understanding, not to hammer the employee with your greater wisdom or higher authority. Share your decisions and your reasons for them. If your decision is final, the employee needs to know.

Employees have ideas and opinions. Don't let those thoughts disappear into a black hole in your office. (Yes, that's a cliché, but it's a good comparison here. Sometimes the gravitational force of management can absorb the brightness of employees, which then disappears without effect.)

If you don't listen and respond, employees will soon stop talking. They won't waste your time or their own. They will start to become dissatisfied and disengaged.

Remember to communicate *with* (not at) your workers. Practice the art of powerful listening, so that you can coach more effectively and make better, more informed decisions.

The Coach's Checklist for Chapter 6

☑ A good coach knows when to step into level 2 listening and then level 3 listening (coach position) to foster a creative environment for problem solving.

☑ Coaching means you have to listen to what employees say. The *seven keys to effective listening* are to (1) be prepared, (2) drop everything else you're doing, (3) maintain eye contact, (4) hear it all before responding, (5) take notes, (6) acknowledge feelings, and (7) allow for silence.

☑ Remember the three Rs of listening: receive, reflect, and rephrase.

Creating Solutions Through Coaching

I n basketball, it all comes down to 40 minutes on the court.

A recruiter finds the players. The conference schedules the games and playoffs. The coach and assistant coaches train and develop the players. The sports analysts and commentators describe and even predict the games. The fans cheer wildly. But when it comes down to it, the game is played by 10 people on the court for 40 minutes. Those players have to make split-second decisions and reactions, with the responsibility of winning or losing on their shoulders. They need the support of all those around them, but only the players on the floor create the results.

The same holds true for business. No matter how well you've laid out policies and procedures, the players on the floor (employees) are the ones who make it happen.

From the hourly temp filing documents and the kid dunking a basket of fries into hot grease to middle- and upper-level managers, workers make dozens of crucial decisions every day. And they have to make them on the run.

You'll do some of your best coaching (especially with teams) when you run with them, working out solutions and anticipating problems together.

THE LESS CONTROL, THE BETTER

SMART

MANAGING

"My people won't make a move without me," Paul brags. "I make sure they check everything with me first." He laughs. "In fact, they're flat out afraid not to!"

Instead of bragging, Paul should look for another job. He's not performing well as a manager. He's too busy trying to do everyone else's job.

Maybe you would like to think that the whole works would fall apart if you weren't there to run everything, but you can't afford such self-indulgence. Being "indispensable" is a good move in the job market, but micromanaging and being a control freak is *not* the way to go about it.

Coach workers well so that they're confident to make decisions without you and capable of making good ones. The better the manager, the less control he or she needs over workers.

Most often you won't be there when those critical decisions have to be made. For that reason, you need a well-coached team of workers, capable of making decisions, taking initiative, and solving problems.

How do you put together a high-performing team?

- Hire them carefully.
- Coach them well.
- Give them room to work.

You want to avoid having to spend your time checking and correcting workers (much less doing their jobs for them). Put in that time up front, coaching workers to do the job right the first time, without having you looking over their shoulders.

If you coach them well, empower them, and trust them, you won't have to correct them later.

Six Steps to Effective Problem Solving

In problem-solving sessions (especially with groups), effective managers follow these six steps:

1. Define the opportunity.
2. Define the goal.
3. Create the action plan.
4. Set the evaluation standard.
5. Confirm understanding.
6. Plan the follow-up.

CONVERSATION, NOT DICTATION
Don't be tempted to call a meeting, write the agenda with the six steps to problem solving, and then dictate what is to be done at each step. Follow the steps, but use them as a launching point to ask for contributions from your employees. Let them contribute, collaborate, and become engaged and invested in the solution. Managers are expected to solve problems, and *great* managers listen to their team as they work toward solutions together.

Let's take those steps one by one.

Step 1. Define the opportunity. It may seem like part of a corny and over-used management mantra: a problem is a challenge, a challenge is an opportunity, and an opportunity is a triumph. In any case, defining the opportunity really does help you create solutions if you look at any situation as a challenge or an opportunity rather than as a crisis or a problem.

Whatever you call it, you and your staff need to know exactly what you're working on. Sometimes that means you, as the coach, need to do a lot of asking and a lot of listening. "How?" questions (How can we move forward? How can we improve? How can we make it even better?) are your best tools here.

You may go into a coaching conversation believing that the problem at hand is Frank's rotten attitude and lack of motivation. By the time you're done asking and listening, you've redefined the problem (with input from Frank) as a lack of meaningful work for Frank to do. Here's an

APOLLO 13
FOR EXAMPLE A simple yet profound example of viewing a problem as an opportunity (and then a triumph) was portrayed movingly in the film *Apollo 13*. After the problems of the seriously damaged spacecraft became apparent, a senior director at NASA said, "This could be the worse disaster NASA's ever faced." To this, flight director Gene Kranz firmly said, "With all due respect, sir, I believe this is gonna be our finest hour."

Kranz was right. Although the crew of Apollo 13 never completed their mission of going to and landing on the moon, they successfully and brilliantly addressed a series of unexpected problems, using the brains and creativity of everyone in orbit and on the ground in Mission Control. The astronauts came home safely, which was against all expectations and odds.

opportunity to put Frank where he can contribute more value to the company and find greater job satisfaction.

Make sure everybody involved has a clear and consistent sense of the opportunity before you move on to step 2. Once they can perceive what's going on in terms of an opportunity (instead of a problem or crisis), the momentum to move forward toward a solution will be significant.

Step 2. Define the goal. Once you get the opportunity mapped out, the goal usually seems obvious. But that's often only in appearance. Let's take an example.

You're not selling enough harpsichords. You should sell more harpsichords, right? Of course. But to whom, and for what purpose?

Do you go back to your old customers, trying to persuade them to buy another harpsichord or two? If so, for what reason? Do you have a new use for your product? ("The harpsichord—your musical salami slicer.") How about a new occasion to use it in the same old way? ("The harpsichord: it's not just for after dinner anymore.")

Do you try to open up a new market? If so, how will you identify and reach those people? Why aren't they buying from you already?

"We need to sell more harpsichords" isn't a clear enough goal.

Let's try, "We need to develop a market for harpsichords among the nearly 200,000 owners of Harley-Davidson motorcycles in our marketing area." That's better. (It may be nuts, but it is a lot more specific.)

As you start to clarify your goal, make sure it is SMART. SMART goals are optimized for success, because they are

- Specific
- Measurable
- Achievable
- Realistic
- Timed for completion

The goal for selling harpsichords in a new market is getting clearer, but can be even more specific. A SMART version of it might read: "We will sell 2,000 harpsichords in the first half of the next fiscal year to Harley-Davidson owners in this metropolitan area with a targeted marketing campaign." Is it SMART? Let's check.

- Specific: 2,000 harpsichords sold (yes, very specific), also in a very specific market (Harley owners in this metropolitan area).
- Measurable: yes—the sales numbers will indicate how many harpsichords are sold, and marketing data will track the effect of promotional efforts. You'll know definitively whether you achieved this goal.
- Achievable: probably, because your target audience is clearly outlined and the sales number is not astronomical. (If you wanted to sell harpsichords to citizens of Mars, however, this goal would not pass the "achievable" test.)
- Realistic: Yes. (You might not pass the "realistic" test if you wanted to sell a harpsichord to *every* Harley owner in the area, or if there were only 500 of them.)
- Timed for completion: Yes, a six-month timeline is clearly indicated, with start and end dates (beginning of fiscal year to mid-year, which may vary depending on the fiscal calendar used by the company).

SMART GoALS

SMART goals aren't only for business strategies. They can be applied anywhere a particular outcome is desired: personal goals, professional development, even New Year's resolutions. Using the SMART acronym can turn a pie-in-the-sky dream into a reality. Here's the list again, for easy reference:

TOOLS

- Specific
- Measurable
- Achievable
- Realistic
- Timed for completion

A bridge step between defining the goal and getting to the action plan is to *create the action statement. How* are you going to market those harpsichords to Harley owners? You need an action statement.

The action statement recasts the definition of the goal and explains in broad terms how it will be achieved: "We will sell 2,000 harpsichords in the first half of the next fiscal year to Harley-Davidson owners in this metropolitan area with a targeted marketing campaign that includes sponsoring events, social media marketing, direct mail, and live in-store promotional events."

Step 3. Create the action plan. Look at your action statement part of your goal: "a targeted marketing campaign that includes sponsoring events, social media marketing, direct mail, and live in-store promotional events." This statement includes the seeds of your actual action steps. Break it down: What action steps happen to begin sponsoring events? You might brainstorm that this involves finding national, regional, and local events; approaching organizers about sponsorship and promotional opportunities; putting together materials to give to attendees of these events; and a follow-up and data tracking plan. Social media marketing will break down into such steps as creating a Facebook fan page, a blog, and Twitter ID; hiring writers to provide content; developing special promotions to be delivered this way; and tracking data.

Brainstorm with your team, throw out all the ideas you have, then start picking among them to create a doable plan.

Don't adjourn the meeting until you've got a specific plan—if not the entire process, at least the first few steps and who is responsible for what. Everyone should leave with a clear idea of what they're supposed to do next and how soon they're supposed to do it.

Step 4. Set the evaluation standard. How will you know if you've achieved your goal? This is called the *evidence procedure*. If your goal is SMART, you've made sure it's specific, and therefore you'll know unequivocally whether you've achieved it.

It's amazing how often people launch action plans without considering how to investigate the value of each step or the overall plan. Many people forget to check with the overall goal, and simply assume that when a particular action step is done, they have achieved the goal. It's important for each action step to have its own evaluation standard, so its effectiveness can be judged.

If the action step is simply a canvass of every Harley-Davidson owner in the area, then a chart, a timeline, and a marking pen are all the evaluation tools you need. When you've checked every name off the chart, you're finished.

If you expect something to happen as a *result* of this action step, evaluation becomes a bit trickier. Define the desired result qualitatively and quantitatively. What do you want the Harley-Davidson owners to *do* as a result of the action? Send for more information? Sign up for a free trial harpsichord lesson? Give you a down payment? How many of them do you need to get to do it for the action to be considered a success (or, conversely, at what point is the payoff not worth the effort)?

For instance, if you track the social media campaign marketing harpsichords to Harley owners, you might decide that you want sales of 300 units from these efforts alone. You find that the blog gets the most readership (tracked with online analytics), but other media efforts really help boost awareness, which drives attendance at events and word-of-mouth, and the total for sales resulting from this category of action is 400 units. You also realized that the costs to implement this campaign were fairly low. Perhaps you only need sales of 40 units to simply break even, so you learn the profit margin from these efforts was particularly high.

TRICKS OF THE TRADE

TRACKING RESULTS

If you want to *change* it, you have to *track* it. Evaluation is critical before, during, and after changes. You can quantify your results and identify useful learning if you track the details along the way. Create evaluations for each goal, action plan, and even qualitative change you want to see. Showing the quantitative payoff for action and change demonstrates value, which is always important in the workplace.

Step 5. Confirm understanding. Before you end the session, make sure that everyone has a clear understanding of what has been decided. Ask them to repeat key points to you, especially their areas of responsibility.

Step 6. Plan the follow-up. Make sure everyone has specific marching orders and a time for the next session, if any. Don't leave it open-ended. The follow-up plan to a particular meeting might look like this:

- Dave types up the draft memo and gets it out by e-mail to the rest of the group by the next morning.
- Every unit manager gets his or her input on the draft back to Dave by noon.
- Dave sends out a final draft by 3 p.m.
- Managers circulate the memo to members of their divisions and get as much feedback as possible.

- The group meets again in one week (same time, same place) to compare responses and draft the final report.

  Follow-up also offers an important aspect: *accountability.* If people know what the next step is and when it's due, they have a deadline for jumping into their action plan. Action steps that are not scheduled or followed up on will continually be pushed away in favor of more urgent projects and items.

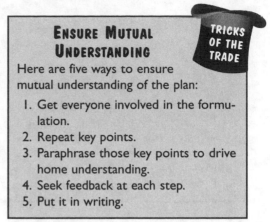

ENSURE MUTUAL UNDERSTANDING

Here are five ways to ensure mutual understanding of the plan:

1. Get everyone involved in the formulation.
2. Repeat key points.
3. Paraphrase those key points to drive home understanding.
4. Seek feedback at each step.
5. Put it in writing.

Solution-Focused Coaching

There are many different "flavors" and niches of coaching (coactive coaching, spiritual coaching, career coaching, and so on), and one of the most popular and broadly applicable kinds is known as *solution-focused coaching.* At its essence, this powerful technique is about focusing on the desired state or goal and working to achieve it. As a manager, you have many ways to apply solution-focused coaching with your employees, and it works extremely well in one-on-one sessions.

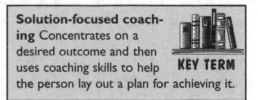

Solution-focused coaching Concentrates on a desired outcome and then uses coaching skills to help the person lay out a plan for achieving it.

KEY TERM

The previous six steps of effective problem solving definitely come into play, and you can combine them with solution-focused coaching techniques.

The essence of a coaching session that is focused on solutions comes down to four main questions:

1. What do you want?
2. Why is it important?
3. How will you get it?
4. How will you stay accountable?

FOUR QUESTIONS CHECKLIST

TOOLS These four questions can serve to open up many possibilities and frequently form the heart of most coaching sessions:

1. What do you want?
2. Why is it important?
3. How will you get it?
4. How will you stay accountable?

Let's look at each of these questions in turn.

1. What do you want? This is a key coaching question. As we have mentioned earlier, never assume that you know why someone is coming to you or what they want to talk about. You may have an inkling of what's up, but let them define the topic in their own terms. This question elicits responses that help define the opportunity and the goal (remember to help the employee make it a SMART goal).

2. Why is it important? Although this question may not appear in the six steps to problem solving, it can be critical in helping someone find personal motivation to make a change. Sometimes this question throws people off, so another way to word it is "What will that do for you?" Help the other person go big! How would achieving their goal pay off for them personally, and how would others (their coworkers, the department, the company) be affected?

For instance, if Bob has the goal of learning to be a better speaker, the payoff might be that he makes more money (through sales commissions and bonuses), which allows him to afford a trip to Europe on his next big

SMART

COACHABLE MOMENTS

MANAGING Take advantage of coachable moments to bring out the best in your employees. For instance, a great time to try solution-focused coaching is during a 360 evaluation or performance review. The employee should be looking ahead to set goals and improve on the previous year's performance. Asking the solution-focused coaching questions helps him or her specify the goal, find a deeper motivation for it, and lay out an action plan.

vacation, something he has always dreamed of doing. Suddenly, a work action has a significant personal payoff. In addition, his coworkers might respect him more and model his behavior, and the whole department increases sales, which leads to recognition from the company and the opportunity for promotions and bonuses.

3. How will you get it? This is where the raw brainstorming and creativity start to flow, similar to developing an action statement. As the ideas start to come forth, the employee will start narrowing down which ones to implement or try out (the action plan step). This is a good opportunity for creating back-up plans, too, in case something gets off track. For instance, a planned family leave or unplanned sick leave (due to illness or injury) might seriously derail an action plan. Having alternatives in mind can be helpful (although limited, as we can't possibly see all potential disruptions).

4. How will you stay accountable? This is a very important question, especially in one-on-one coaching and for personal goals. Some people are very accountable to themselves and work hard to meet their responsibilities. Others need support. Sometimes, a regular coaching session (say, once a week) is enough for someone to stay accountable, if he or she has to report to the coach whether the previous action steps were done. Other options for accountability include finding a "buddy" to work with or report to (say, if the goal was to start running regularly, finding a running buddy might be helpful) or giving oneself a reward of some kind when various benchmarks are reached.

DANGLING THE CARROT

I once had a coaching client who loved to get pedicures. She decided to use this as her motivational carrot to complete her action items. If she met all her commitments and completed her action steps from the session, she allowed herself to get a pedicure at her favorite spa. It became a code question with us at our sessions. I would ask "What color are your toes?" If she responded with a different color than the week or two before, then I knew she had met her commitments.

Your employees can decide on the appropriate "carrot" to dangle that motivates them, so be sure to ask them. It might be a pedicure, it might be a fancy latte, or it might be that raise they've been wanting.

Degrees of Difficulty

We just presented a formal process for creating solutions and some techniques for one-on-one solution-focused coaching. We stressed up-front planning and discussion, with clear communication and feedback to remove misunderstandings, before the job begins. We also offered techniques for finding motivation, creativity, and accountability.

Now we offer some examples of how issues of various degrees of difficulty might be handled with these processes.

Low Degree of Difficulty: The Clogged Commode

"Hey, boss! The toilet's backed up in the men's bathroom."

"Well, let's unplug it."

"You want me to call a plumber?"

"No. We can handle this. There's a plunger in the utility closet off the entryway. If that doesn't work, we've got a snake in the basement."

"By 'we,' you mean 'me,' right?"

"Yeah."

"Okay. I'll get to it right after I finish the . . ."

"You'd better do this first."

"Yeah. I guess you're right."

"Let me know when you're done. If you have any problems, give a holler."

Believe it or not, even this simple exchange follows the six-step process. Take another look. They're all there (more or less).

1. Define the opportunity. "The toilet's backed up in the men's bathroom."
2. Define the goal. Unplug the toilet. Also, the action statement was created: "You want me to call a plumber?"
   "No. We can handle this."
3. Create the action plan. "There's a plunger in the utility closet off the entryway. If that doesn't work, we've got a snake in the basement."
   "By 'we,' you mean 'me,' right?"
4. Set the evaluation standard. Again, this is implied. When the toilet flushes freely, you've reached the goal.
5. Confirm understanding. "Okay. I'll get to it right after I finish the . . ."
   5a. Clarify confirmation. "You'd better do this first."
   5b. Reconfirmation. "Yeah. I guess you're right."
6. Plan the follow-up. "Let me know when you're done. If you have any problems, give a holler."

A lot of the steps of solution-focused coaching were also covered, although very implicitly and without a lot of give-and-take in this situation (not *every* situation requires coaching!). "What do you want?" is implied (a free-flushing toilet in the men's room). "Why is it important?" is also not spelled out but is fairly clear (generally, you want to avoid a mess and a major repair). How to go about it is very clear: options include calling a plumber, using a plunger, or getting the plumbing snake. The options are narrowed down to using the plunger, with the snake as a back-up. "How will you stay accountable?" is also clearly delineated, by letting the boss know when you are done.

Nothing to it, right? At least, not at this low level of difficulty, with a simple, clear-cut problem.

Medium Degree of Difficulty: The Personnel Pigsty

1. Define the opportunity. You've gotten a lot of complaints about the break room. Folks are leaving dirty coffee mugs in the sink, nobody's cleaning the coffee filter, and the pot hasn't been washed since the invention of decaf. There are little live things trying to creep out of the refrigerator. The door of the microwave has crusted shut.

2. Define the goal. At a monthly department meeting, your group quickly reaches consensus on the goal—get the place cleaned up before you have to hire a bulldozer and level it.

Next, create the action statement. Agreement is a lot harder at this stage. In fact, discussion gets rather heated. Some potential solutions are presented:

- "Naming no names, but the whole mess is being generated by just a few. I say we make them clean it up!" [That suggestion generates a rather strenuous discussion.]
- "I say leave it as it is. If people want to wallow in a pigsty, let 'em." [This suggestion is greeted by a chorus of "Right on!"]
- "Circulate a memo outlining a policy on cleanliness, with clear penalties for noncompliance." [This is met with widespread groans and scattered hooting.]
- "Hire a cleaning service." [General cheers.]
- "Shut it down. If people can't behave properly, they don't deserve the privilege of a break room." [The person making the suggestion is invited to swig poison.]

■ "Make the brass use the same room as the rest of us. They'd make sure it got cleaned up soon enough." [Laughter.]

■ "Why not just rotate the duty? Have a sign-up list for making the coffee and cleaning the pot. Everybody washes their own mugs. We clean our stuff out of the refrigerator on the last Friday of the month. Last one out unplugs. We rotate who cleans it out the following Monday." [Silence. A few nods. "Yeah. That makes sense," someone mutters. An action statement is born.]

Refine the action statement. When someone says, "I never use the break room. Why should I have to clean it?" You respond, "Good point. We'll limit the clean-up duty and coffee making to the people who use the room."

3. Create the action plan. Here's where a good, simple plan can fall apart. Everyone agrees on it. With the best of intentions, they leave the meeting, confident that "we'll get that break room cleaned up now." Then nobody does anything because a clear action plan with responsibilities has not been outlined.

In the absence of volunteers (a common situation, unfortunately), you'll assume the leadership role, appointing someone to make the sign-up list (or doing it yourself) and getting things going. (Try to resist the natural temptation to automatically select the person who came up with the suggestion. You want to encourage innovation, remember?)

4. Set the evaluation standard. Does somebody have to be "in charge"? That's a tough question. Human nature being what it is, if everybody is equally responsible, then nobody's really responsible. But avoid setting anybody up as a "cleanliness cop"—especially you. Let the users set the standards; if it's good enough for the folks who take their breaks there, it's good enough. Nobody said anything about bringing in placemats and cloth napkins.

5. Confirm understanding. "Okay, Francisco. You're going to post the sign-up list and take coffee duty for the first week, right? We'll all get our stuff out of the fridge by Friday afternoon, or else it gets pitched. I'll take first crack at mucking the thing out Monday."

6. Plan the follow-up. "Let's give it a month to see how it works out. At our next meeting, we'll decide if it's working."

High Degree of Difficulty: The Thumb Drive Conundrum

A play in one act with two roles—the Coach (you) and the Assistant (Connie).

You've got half a warehouse full of 8 GB thumb drives.

"I guess I overordered," Connie says.

You mentally note that she doesn't make excuses or try to pass the buck.

"Looks like it," you acknowledge, "or else we undersold. Either way, we've got an opportunity on our hands."

Connie grins. She's used to

> **DON'T FORGET TO "DO IT!"** **CAUTION**
>
> There's a very important final step we haven't talked about yet. After "Plan the follow-up" must come "Do it!"
>
> You've got to follow through on the follow-up. If necessary, use sticky note reminders, calendar notations, and computer tickler messages to remind you of what you promised to do and when you said you would do it.
>
> If you don't follow through on the follow-up, nobody's going to play along next time. You talk the talk, but you must also walk the walk.

you using words like "opportunity" when you really mean "monumental screw-up," but it still makes her smile.

"What should we do?" she asks.

You fend off the initial flood of anxiety that comes naturally to all of us who have been trained to believe in the doctrine of management infallibility. It's taken a while, but you've learned better. The boss doesn't always have the answer. But the coach can help create one.

"Let's talk about it," you suggest. "What do you think we should do?"

Connie's used to this approach, too. She's not scared or defensive, thinking you're just turning the gun back on her. She knows you intend to help her.

In the next five minutes of discussion, you quickly decide on the goal—to get rid of all those drives (the "what do you want?" part of solution-focused coaching)—and a secondary goal—to avoid making the company look foolish for ordering too many of them (the "why is it important?" component, although you can certainly come up with more reasons).

Getting to the action statement takes a little longer. Your discussion generates these possibilities, among others:

- Get loyal customers to use more thumb drives by creating a marketing campaign (possibly with a celebrity endorsement) based around being organized and having multiple backups.
- Soak the drives in some mild corrosive so that the USB contacts break easily, rendering them useless after one or two plug-ins.
- Slash the price of the drives drastically, or use them as value-added giveaways to other products.
- Take a page from the baking soda people and create new uses for the thumb drives—as high-tech Legos, fashion accessory, MP3 player, and so on.
- Burn the warehouse and claim the insurance.

You settle on a solution. You'll launch a celebrity testimonial campaign, using Leo Laporte, well-respected technology analyst, as your spokesperson. As fate would have it, Leo uses a *lot* of thumb drives. Your slogan: "Leo gets it right!"

Once you've decided on your solution, it's a downhill ride as you frame your action plan and means of evaluation, confirm your understanding, and schedule the follow-up.

The more you use these techniques of problem solving and solution-focused coaching, the more you're likely to find that the solution isn't

MAKE BRAINSTORMING WORK

When you're brainstorming for solutions,

- Don't discuss the merits of any solution until you're sure you've created as many possibilities as you can. The focus should be on creativity, not critical analysis, and providing quantity, not ensuring quality.
- Separate the idea from the person who proposed it. You want to discuss possibilities, not personalities. Let others build on and modify any ideas proposed. Not only does this approach lead to better ideas, it also encourages the whole group to assume ownership of them. That makes it easier to implement whatever ideas seem best.
- Ruining the thumb drives is clearly a hare-brained idea, slashing prices or giving them away may not be feasible (the profit margin being rather slender), and you wouldn't really become a party to insurance fraud. But you should note each idea and go on to another.

By the way, it's okay to laugh—if the idea is intended to be funny. It may even be a good idea, breaking any tension. However, never laugh at serious suggestions. Nothing can kill a creative mood faster than ridicule.

DON'T RUSH YOUR DECISIONS

CAUTION

You might not have to make a decision immediately, and it might be a good idea if you don't rush it.

The bigger the opportunity, and the more that's at stake, the more likely it is that you'll want to defer a decision until a second coaching session. That gives everyone time to seek feedback, do some research, and generate more ideas, of course. It also gives the subconscious mind a chance to mull things over—and possibly give you (or anyone else on your team) one of those wonderful middle-of-the-night "Aha!" revelations.

---

really the major challenge. You're apt to encounter the highest hurdles when you try to define the *opportunity*.

Let's look at another example.

Sales personnel at your retail outlets don't seem to be sensitive to fluctuations in the pricing structure. (Translation: They aren't changing the prices when you tell them to.) That's what doctors would call the "presenting symptom," like a bad rash or a persistent cough.

What's at the heart of the problem here? There are three possibilities:

1. You've got idiots for salespeople. If so, you should have other evidence of the idiocy. Heart of the problem: The wrong people were hired.

2. They have some reason for defying the "edict from on high." That possibility might be worth talking about. Heart of the problem: The sales force is unmotivated or even demoralized.

3. They aren't getting the word when you think they are. Heart of the problem: a breakdown in the line of communications.

WHERE IS THE LEARNING?

SMART
MANAGING

As you look back on opportunities that came from "problems" and evaluate your solutions, be sure to note where learning occurred. This is critical for moving ahead in business. If a problem arose, find out *how* it happened. For instance, did the thumb drives not sell because the market for them shifted to online cloud computing, or were more people using their smart phones for data storage? Did Connie or the vendor simply misplace a decimal in the order or add in a zero? These details can be incredibly useful in future planning. After the solution has been implemented, find out what was learned. If Leo Laporte promoted the new thumb drives on his multiple podcasts, how many were sold? How many new customers did the company get, and what other products were sold to them? Was this a worthwhile investment that should be continued or repeated?

Put your money on the third possibility—though you might need to do a bit of investigation of the other possibilities as well as options for correcting the problem before you move on to the action stages.

You're currently getting the word out on prices through a confidential bulletin, which goes out via e-mail the last Thursday of every month, and there's a monthly conference call with regional managers of the retail outlets. The salespeople should be getting the information pretty much immediately, which gives them some time to implement changes before your deadline of the seventh of the next month.

In case the bulletins are getting lost, delayed, or bounced back, and managers skip the conference calls, you start faxing the notices, but nothing improves.

GET THEM WORKING WITH YOU

As in *Animal Farm*, all people in the company are equal, but you as manager are "more equal" than Connie. As an enlightened coach, you know it's a lot more productive to encourage Connie to work *with* you rather than for you.

You and Connie created the solution together. If the "Leo gets it right!" campaign succeeds, you'll share the glory. In fact, as a wise coach, you'll step aside and let your player have the spotlight. (After all, the better she looks, the better you look.) If the idea flops, don't let Connie take the fall. Now's the time for you to step forward and shoulder the responsibility. Remember: a worker is responsible, but the manager is *accountable*.

You haven't given that responsibility away by coaching. You couldn't, even if you wanted to. It's still your call. You just reached your decision in a better way—better because collaboration helps employees develop, and better because you had more input before you made it.

A little sleuthing reveals that the salespeople aren't *reading* your bulletin. (It has, in fact, become the ultimate "confidential" bulletin: Nobody knows what's in it.) Many of them weren't even aware that they were receiving it. In an e-mail inbox filled with spam, it's hard to spot the important messages. Some managers still don't process their e-mail in a timely way.

Now you're ready to brainstorm solutions. You might pursue "ways to get them to read the bulletin." (Redesign. Bribery. Pop quizzes tied to salary adjustments.) By limiting yourself to that focus, you ignore the broader question: Is an e-mail bulletin the best way to communicate this information? How else might you do it? Ask the people involved.

Asking the right people the right questions is the essence of good coaching. You'll get your players involved in the process, you'll get a better answer, and they'll all own that answer when it comes time to put it into practice. And that generally means less effort.

Structure problem-solving sessions so that everyone participates in creating the solution, and everyone is clear about who does what to make it work. Use solution-focused coaching one on one to tap the creativity and potential of your employees.

CREATE THE SOLUTION   SMART

You're not looking for the "right answer." You're creating a solution you will all act on together.   **MANAGING**

Seeking the "right answer" will prevent you from being able to settle on any solution. Letting go of being "right" or finding "the best" answer can free you up to evaluate many options and find value.

Creating solutions may well be your most important—and most challenging and stimulating—role as coach. You have other crucial functions, which we discuss in the next three chapters.

The Coach's Checklist for Chapter 7

☑ An important goal of a good coach is to help people learn how to solve problems on their own. To do that, you should hire them carefully, coach them well, and then give them room to work.

☑ Here's an effective six-step methodology for coaching employees to solve problems: (1) define the opportunity (problems are always opportunities in disguise), (2) define the goal, (3) create the action plan (with an action statement), (4) set the evaluation standard, (5) confirm understanding, and (6) plan the follow-up.

☑ Solution-focused coaching works well in one-on-one sessions with employees. You'll ask what they want, why it's important, how they will get it, and how they will stay accountable.

☑ Understand, as a coach, how to apply this methodology to problems of different levels of complexity.

The Coach
as Trainer

L et's start with three images.

First, imagine a lion tamer. Confronting those wild cats, a chair in one hand and a whip in the other, a lion tamer thrusts and lunges, the lions roar and claw, and then the tamer gets those huge hunks of ferocity to sit up on chairs, roll over, and otherwise shame their heritage.

Second, a frequent scene from the Westerns has cowpokes sitting on the fence, watching one veteran bronc buster after another get thrown by a raging mustang.

"Nobody can break Fury," one grizzled vet asserts.

"Bet I could," says the fuzzy-cheeked new kid.

The camera cuts to the kid, clinging to the infuriated horse that's whirling, bucking, trying to scrape the kid off on the railing, all but jumping out of its hide in its efforts to throw its rider.

The kid, of course, breaks Fury, earning the grudging respect of the rest of the cowboys.

Finally, a grizzled drill instructor confronts a new crop of recruits. Disgust floods his face as he walks up and down the line of ragtag misfits, which he must, of course, shape into an efficient fighting machine.

Most of the recruits look scared. One wears a smirk.

"Something funny?" the DI asks, getting in the recruit's face.

"No," the cocky kid replies, adding "Sir" a beat too late.

The DI rides the kid mercilessly, singling him out for physical punishment and verbal abuse.

The kid takes everything the DI can dish out and, in the process, learns to become *a man*.

Why begin this chapter on the coach as trainer with the images of a lion tamer, a horse breaker, and a drill instructor? Only to reject them as examples of training. When we talk about your role as a trainer, we don't mean taming lions, breaking horses, or molding raw recruits into Marines.

Don't confront the trainee with a whip and a chair. Don't get on the trainee's back. Don't get in the trainee's face.

One more image, common to us all: the teacher holding forth behind the lectern at the front of the classroom, carried away by the sound of his or her own voice, while all the students nod off. Nope. That's not an ideal image either.

Come out from behind the podium. Stand shoulder to shoulder with the learner. Only then will you be ready to teach and train—and learn.

As a manager, you are probably responsible (to a certain degree) for training your team of employees. They may need to know how to do their tasks, or you may need to teach them about new company policies, initiatives, and procedures. You may have already done a lot of training or presentations and feel confident in those skills.

Adding a coach approach to your training skills can make you far more effective as a teacher and help you connect to your trainees on a deeper level. You can encourage real learning by bringing in a few coaching techniques.

Guidelines for the Coach as Trainer

The first requirement to be an effective trainer is mastery of the task or knowledge. It's fairly common today for top management to bring in a supervisor from another area to take over an operation. Some supervisors receive only management training and join an organization without being familiar with the products, services, or processes involved.

IT'S OKAY NOT TO KNOW

Maybe you've heard this advice: Don't ever let on that you don't know. Nonsense.

Too many managers try to hide massive ignorance behind slender knowledge. It's like trying to hide an elephant behind a palm tree.

Employees figure out soon enough that you don't know what you're doing (or not as much as they do). You're a lot better off letting them know that you know it—and that you're willing to learn. Don't be afraid to ask "ignorant" questions. The only truly ignorant question is the one you won't let yourself ask because you're worried about looking bad.

Be open about your ignorance. Just don't *remain* in it. It's okay to say "I don't know—but I'll find out!"

If you find yourself in this position, your first job is to learn before you teach. Take every training opportunity that presents itself and that you can seek out, including informal on-the-job training. Read. Observe. Ask questions. Do your homework. Don't be too proud to ask those who work "for" you to become your teachers.

You have a great opportunity for self-coaching here. Figure out what you want to know about, set a timeline for when you want to know it, seek out learning opportunities, and track your progress.

Simply knowing the job isn't enough to enable you to teach it effectively. You need to have presentation and training skills to transmit knowledge to others.

The first guideline for good teaching, then, involves what you do *before* you start.

Prepare to Present

A coach approach to preparing for training focuses on the *learner*. What do you want the other person (or people) to *know*? What are the key goals of the training? How do your employees learn best (being told, being shown, being allowed to do)? How do you teach best?

Think through the process or material you're going to teach. Break it down into steps. Keep things as simple and direct as you can, and be careful not to skip anything. If you've done the task for a long time, you may not even think about some of the steps involved. Approach it from the point of view of someone new to the task, the machinery, or the process.

THE 3x5 CARD TRICK

Jot key steps in a process (or key talking points) on a 3x5 index card. If the process won't fit, either simplify your explanation or divide the process into simpler subprocesses on other cards. When trainees master the subprocesses, they've also mastered the whole process.

It may seem technologically outdated to use index cards instead of a slide presentation but consider this: Technology doesn't always work on demand. Index cards don't need a working projector, laptop, thumb drive, or WiFi connection.

TRICKS OF THE TRADE

As you start planning the training, keep a few preparation steps in mind. After adopting a learning-centered mindset and thinking about the processes you'll be teaching, you may need to do some more research and outlining. Perform necessary research you need to do ahead of time. Then develop your outline, keeping it as simple as possible. Start filling out your content once you have an outline ready.

When developing your content, use simple, direct language. If workers need to know technical terms, use and explain those terms. If they don't need them, don't bring them up. Give them what *they* need—not what you want to teach. Rehearse your presentation. No matter how well you know the process, you need to practice explaining it. Go over the steps in your mind several times—first thing when you wake up, on your way to work, and again a few minutes before you start the training. If you have limited time, say a one-hour teleconference call or 90 minutes in a meeting room, rehearse with a stopwatch so that you know whether you are respecting the time limits. The more you rehearse, the less you'll need your notes.

Practice key words and phrases you'll need to use and any statistics you need to cite.

Anticipate questions and practice answers. (If you get a

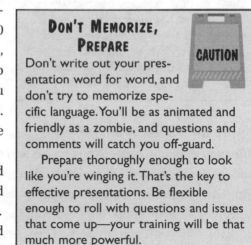

DON'T MEMORIZE, PREPARE

CAUTION

Don't write out your presentation word for word, and don't try to memorize specific language. You'll be as animated and friendly as a zombie, and questions and comments will catch you off-guard.

Prepare thoroughly enough to look like you're winging it. That's the key to effective presentations. Be flexible enough to roll with questions and issues that come up—your training will be that much more powerful.

question you can't handle, admit that you don't have an answer and make it your business to get one as soon as possible.)

Even five minutes of this kind of rehearsal pays real dividends in terms of your ability to communicate clearly and to get your trainees up and running at the level you expect.

Prepare to Demonstrate

You've got it all over a training manual or demonstration tape. You can get feedback, verbal and nonverbal, and you can answer questions. You can watch workers try things and see how well they understand. Most important, you can put your hands on the equipment and *show* while you tell.

Some learners do well with auditory learning (listening), others do better with visual learning (being shown), and some prefer kinesthetic (movement, hands-on) techniques. If you can use more than one technique (or all three), you'll not only reach all your trainees, you'll reinforce their learning.

RESOURCES

TOOLS To improve your presentation skills, check out *Presentation Skills for Managers*, by Jennifer Rotondo and Mike Rotondo Jr. (Briefcase Books, 2001). For hands-on practice, investigate Toastmasters International (www.toastmasters .org), a widely recognized organization dedicated to helping individuals improve public speaking and leadership skills.

Work through the demonstration at least once and preferably a few times before you attempt it for trainees. If possible, work on the same equipment you'll use for the demonstration. Be prepared for technology failures with hard-copy backups of material you'll need (handouts, outlines, etc.).

Apply the KYHO Principle

After you've demonstrated the process and answered questions, step aside and let the trainees do it. Resist the temptation to do it for them the first time they falter. Stick to the Keep Your Hands Off (KYHO) principle. Answer questions. Give prompts. But keep your hands clasped behind your back.

Don't show off your mastery. The teacher isn't the star—even though you might have the spotlight on you for a while. The *learner* is the focus.

If the demonstration does not seem to be working for your trainees, take a few deep breaths, think through the process, and try it again. Let your trainees in on the fun. "Okay, guys. What am I doing wrong here?" Don't try to fake it. Say, "I just did that to see if you were paying attention" only if that's really the case. Listen to their responses. They will tell you what makes sense, what doesn't. You can then respond in support of their learning.

ENABLE THEM

They haven't truly learned it until they can do it without you.

Your job as a trainer is to teach employees. Your job as a manager is to enable them to do it.

It's all in the application. In your childhood, you watched somebody else drive a car. Then the motor vehicle department gave you a manual to study. That wasn't enough. You learned how to drive with someone beside you. That still wasn't enough. When you actually became able to drive by yourself, that was what really mattered.

Also be aware that true learning takes practice. After you tell, show, and even let them do it once, they will still need practice until they are sure of themselves. Don't expect 100 percent mastery as soon as the class is done. Be ready to support your trainees as needed, again, letting *them* do the learning.

Train for Small Successes

Teach enough, but not too much.

Don't parcel out information in such small doses that they must keep coming back to you for each new step. ("As soon as you've logged into the intranet, I'll come back and show you how to fill out this sales form.") This fosters dependence, slows the learning, and frustrates learners. Give them enough information to let them carry out a process without you being there. Let them get into the process quickly enough to experience and appreciate it.

It's the difference between making beginning guitar students practice three chords over and over for weeks and teaching them to play a simple three-chord song. The first approach is boring and frustrating. The second is fun (which is why they call it "playing," not "working" the guitar).

SMART

MANAGING

LET THEM FIGURE IT OUT
When employees stumble at a task, resist the temptation to do it for them or even tell them immediately what they did wrong and what they should do. Instead, employ the coach's greatest tool—the question. "What do you think went wrong there?" or "How are you going to fix this?" is more effective than "Here, let me show you again." The first approach communicates your confidence in them and keeps the learner actively involved. The second takes the task out of the learner's hands.

But don't load on so much all at once that they're bound to fail. Progress at the pace of the learner. If you're training more than one person, and they're progressing at different rates, separate them if you can, so the faster learner doesn't rush the slower one past important steps, and the slower one doesn't frustrate the speedy learner.

Offer praise and reinforcement if appropriate and if you're comfortable doing it. Keep criticism to a minimum and your comments constructive—focused on how to improve, rather than on what's going wrong. Don't say anything that doesn't seem honest and natural to you. Remember: What you say isn't as important as what you let them do.

Foster Mastery and Independence

Never lose sight of your true goal as a trainer—to focus on other aspects of your job as a manager.

If they walk away from the training session convinced they did it all themselves, fine. You aren't in this to get credit or to keep them dependent on you for training and information. You're in it to coach workers to peak performance, including acquisition of new skills and techniques.

Smile if you hear them say, "I probably could have picked it up faster without any help." They're really saying that you did your job well.

Before, During, and After Training

New hires might come in with experience, certificates, and degrees attesting to their competence. But somehow they don't seem to know what you thought they would.

They, like you, are victims of a changing work world where what we learned yesterday is no longer very helpful today. Your systems may not look anything like what the new hire worked with just a few months ago in school or at his or her previous job. An employee returning to the workplace after a time out for other pursuits may be several generations behind. Therefore, make sure you take the time necessary to address the issues specific to each stage of the process before moving on to the next phase.

Before You Start Training

Explain clearly what the learners are going to do and why they're going to do it. Describe the specific goals. Define the desired outcomes.

If you just dive right in, you're more likely to encounter snags and frustrations. It's harder to do something right if you have to undo something wrong.

Take time here. It will save you time later. Also, by clearly delineating the goals and outcomes, you'll know whether the training was successful.

If you're training several people at a time, you'll also need to kick off the session with some logistics. This may seem minor, but outlining when bathroom breaks can be taken and requesting that everyone silence their cell phones helps keep people focused and on task.

While You Train

Take it one step at a time, demonstrating, observing, commenting. Get feedback from the workers at each step. It's a lot easier and less frustrating to keep them on track than to have to figure out where they are and get them back on track later. If you can adjust your material on the fly, the audience will have a far more satisfying learning experience. Anything interactive you can do (asking questions, role-playing if necessary, getting the trainees involved) will drive home your point and keep attendees attentive.

After You Train

Be ready with feedback for learners, and stay open to questions. Be prepared to get feedback from students on your training method.

Don't assume that because you walked them through it once, they've got it forever. Some people can learn quickly, while others need to go through the process many times.

Don't forget to follow up. Did you have handouts or copies of your slides for trainees? How about a pop quiz? A Q&A session or follow-up

> ### EVALUATION
>
> After any kind of presentation you give—whether it's group train-ing or one-on-one—you would be wise to get some sort of evalu-ation. This could be a comment card, a quick survey, or off-the-cuff comments. Consider a survey that asks people to quantify their experience. Instead of asking "Was this helpful?" you could ask "On a scale of 1 to 5, 1 being not at all helpful and 5 being extremely helpful, how would you rate this training?"
>
> Two more powerful questions to ask are "What else would you like to learn?" and "What could make the training better?"

meeting scheduled? Make sure your employees get what you promise them. This will reinforce their learning, especially if they have written materials to refer to.

Two's Company, Three's a Crowd?

The best training often takes place one-on-one, creating an intense learning experience, which helps explain why some of the most effective training occurs spontaneously on the job. It also explains why you, and not a hired outside trainer, wind up doing a lot of the teaching.

However, in some situations, one-on-one training isn't effective, because there's too much attention on the individual learner, who might become overly self-conscious. That extra attention may not even be nec-essary, especially if the task requires a lot of practice and not much super-vision. Sometimes you'll need to teach employees in groups, not only to save time but because they'll pick it up faster that way. They can then start explaining things to each other, reinforcing their learning and bring-ing you new viewpoints to consider.

Be prepared to deliver training via Webinar, live seminar, conference call, and even podcasting and written materials. The variety of training options available with modern technology makes imparting information easier than ever.

What Kind of Trainer Are You?

You've probably had gruff teachers and jovial teachers, distant teachers and teachers who wanted to be your pal, strict teachers and hang-loose teachers. What kind should you be?

You should be *yourself.* Of course, that means you should be your best self—prepared, focused, attentive. But it also means that you should train in a way that comes naturally to you. There are really only two basic qualities you must have to be a good trainer:

1. You have to know what you're teaching.
2. You have to genuinely care about your students.

No matter how well you've seen a technique work when somebody else used it, if it feels phony to you when you try it, don't do it. Be authentic—it helps others connect to you and feel at ease.

To take a coach approach, reflect on your own skills, capabilities, and values. If you're a good storyteller, then using anecdotes and examples can boost your training abilities. If you're methodical and protocol-oriented, you will be good at outlining a step-by-step process. If you're a natural speaker, then you'll be able to command attention and keep a training session focused on its goals and keep it from getting derailed.

What do you bring to the table? List your skills and abilities, and you'll start to see how they can translate into good training techniques.

Four Stages of Learning

There are four stages to learning as a person moves toward mastering a process. Knowing these stages and being aware of where your employees fall in them will help you be a better trainer (and coach). The stages are:

- Unconscious Incompetence
- Conscious Incompetence
- Conscious Competence
- Unconscious Competence

Let's look at each of these in turn.

Unconscious Incompetence

In this stage, a person is not even aware that he doesn't know something. This is before learning takes place. A good analogy is a preteen who's thinking about driving a car. At age 12, before taking a class or getting behind the wheel, she thinks it will be easy, because she sees her parents driving like it's no big deal. She's not yet aware that driving takes concentration, knowledge of road laws, multitasking of steering and working pedals, plus dealing with all the distractions on the road.

Conscious Incompetence

In this stage, the learner becomes aware that she doesn't know something and has to focus hard on acquiring new information. She is suddenly aware that she doesn't really know what's going on! This might be when a 15-year-old is in Driver's Ed class and starts to realize that driving is a lot more complicated than just turning a wheel. She starts to learn how a car works, when to change the oil, defensive driving techniques, and more. She finally gets to do some practice driving with her instructor and is nearly overwhelmed at how much there is to think about! She drives very slowly and cautiously, even with the encouragement from her teacher.

When you're training employees, they will start at this phase as soon as you begin imparting information. It takes a while at this stage before they feel comfortable moving to the next one. Don't rush them.

Conscious Competence

In this stage, learners are starting to get it! The process or information is coming more easily and naturally, but it still takes deliberate effort to do it right. They are successful, but still need some concentration to get there.

In terms of driving a car, conscious competence would be reached when the student has a lot more practice in the driver's ed car, and even after she gets her learner's permit and can drive while supervised by her parent. She no longer has to remind herself to put on her turn signal or check her mirrors constantly, as these behaviors are becoming more automatic. She is more comfortable driving and is doing a good job.

Conscious competence will be developed in your employees once you release them from training and allow them to go out and *do*. The more hands-on they get, the faster they will reach this stage.

Unconscious Competence

The information has been learned, processed, and internalized. Now it's second nature—the learner doesn't even have to think about it, it's done automatically.

Our driving student has gotten her license and regularly drives a car with no mishaps. She's so good at driving that it's second nature, and she can relax her focus a bit (while still staying attentive). Sometimes, she finds herself at the mall, even though that wasn't where she intended to go!

With enough practice, your employees will reach this stage, where whatever you trained them on is just part of what they do naturally.

The Learner's Point of View

Let's invite your students to tell you what they need from you as you train them in the workplace. Follow these nine simple principles, and everyone will get the most out of every training session.

1. Remove or minimize the distractions. I'll give you my attention while you teach me, but you've got to do your part by eliminating anything that will get in the way. (This is why we recommend covering logistics at the beginning of a session.)

Potential distractions include

- cell phones and text messages
- "buzz" (background noise)
- "flicker" (irrelevant visual stimulus)
- an audience
- need for breaks (snacks, restroom)

2. Respect my intelligence. I'm your learner. You're my coach, trainer, and manager. You know what I need to know and how I should do it. But that doesn't make you smarter than me.

I may be ignorant about this process, but I'm not stupid. There's a big difference. Ignorance is a temporary condition. I can learn—if you'll help me and let me.

Don't talk down to me. Don't lecture me. Don't disrespect me. If you do, I can guarantee that you won't teach me anything because I will shut you out.

3. Respect my time. I know you're busy. You've got all that important manager stuff to do. But I'm busy, too. I've got worker stuff to do, and my stuff is as important to me as your stuff is to you. (This is why we suggest rehearsing with a stopwatch.)

> ### Don't Sell Tickets
> **CAUTION** You may want to involve several learners in the process at the same time. But you don't want to let others stand around and watch while someone else learns. Learners as spectators can pass judgment and inhibit learning—even if they don't say or do anything.
>
> But if everyone is involved, taking his or her turn trying the process, all the learners are in it together, sharing the frustrations and anxieties of learning. Also, they may tend to help each other—maybe in ways that you couldn't imagine—which facilitates learning and builds team spirit.

I've also got a life outside the workplace, just as you do. I want to have time to live and enjoy that life.

I don't resent good training. I need it, and I want to learn. But I do resent unnecessary training, interruptions, and repetition after I've already got it. Don't make me run laps just to keep me busy, coach. Let me get it and get on with it.

4. Take one step at a time. You can do this stuff in your sleep. But to me it's new. So give me the big picture, what it's supposed to look like when it's done, and then let me take it one step at a time.

5. Take small enough steps. Your definition of a "step" might not be the same as mine. Match your pace to mine in the beginning. I'll soon be able to keep up with you.

6. Build on what I know. This process is new to me, but I know a lot about a lot of things.

When you teach me the new intranet reporting system, don't forget that I already know how to use a computer.

When you teach me how to motivate a potential customer, don't forget that I was a customer for a lot of years before I started training to be a salesperson.

Use experience—yours and mine—to teach me. For example, do you handle that foot pedal the same way you feather the clutch on a car? Does the tug I'm supposed to feel when the gear engages feel anything like the way a trout feels on the line when it's mouthing the bait but hasn't swallowed the hook yet?

LEARNING IS NATURAL

Why can't Johnny read? After all, he learned to talk, and that's surely one of the most amazing feats of learning imaginable—and he did it before he knew what learning was.

He listened, he made noises, and he experimented, stringing noises together into "sentences." (Before any of his "words" made sense, he was using punctuation and inflection to make his babble sound like the adult babble around him.)

He began recognizing words and using them to mean the same thing other people meant when they said them. He progressed from "Dada" and "Mama" to "No!" and "Why?" and hundreds of other words, phrases, and thoughts. He loved to listen to stories and to tell stories of his own.

Then the teacher started Johnny over, at the beginning, trying to teach him how to read as if he had no idea how to use language at all.

"Look at Spot. See Spot run. Run Spot run. Funny, funny Spot."

No wonder so many of us had trouble learning how to read in school, even though so few of us had trouble learning how to talk.

I may not understand the physics of jet propulsion, but I know what happens when you blow up a balloon and let it go without tying it off.

If you can explain what I don't know in terms of what I do know, I'll pick it up a lot faster. If you aren't sure how much I know, I've got a simple suggestion: Ask me. Let me show you what I know. If I'm doing it wrong—or in a way you don't want me to use—you'll see that, and we can work on it.

7. Give me lots of feedback. Tell me how I'm doing.

I'd prefer you tell me nicely, with encouragement. You can skip the sarcasm, and you don't have to raise your voice. But however you do it, let me know if I'm doing it the way you want me to.

"Yes" is as important as "no." "Good job!" is just as helpful as "Not that way." Don't overdo the praise, and don't wait until I screw up to talk to me.

Don't just tell me what I'm doing wrong. Tell me how to do it right. In fact, if you just tell me how to do it right, you don't even have to bother telling me I'm wrong.

8. Don't let it get away. If you want me to really remember what we went over, give me another shot at it the same day, ideally about two hours after the first session. That will do me a lot more good than a review next week or even the next day. Reinforcing what I've learned promptly makes it stick.

9. Let it all settle. You did a great job, and I get it—I really do. But it seems to take a while for everything I learn to sink in. Don't make me tackle another new project right away. My subconscious needs to chew on this for a bit before we move on to more new stuff.

An Ideal Training Session

Now that you've heard about learning from your employees, let's take a look at the process again from your point of view, which is similar. The following five steps provide a basic structure for any training session.

Step 1. Lay it all out. Explain the problem and the outcome you want.

Step 2. Get them doing it. The sooner workers get their hands on the task, the more involved they'll be, and the better they'll learn the process.

Step 3. Give feedback as you go. Anticipate and answer questions and guide the process each step of the way. Let them know how they're doing.

Step 4. Give it a rest. Let a tough lesson settle while workers do something relatively unchallenging.

Step 5. Reinforce it. Review the same day. If possible, it's best to review about two hours after the initial training session.

How Will You Know If It Worked?

As with any other task in the workplace, you need a clear definition of what you want to accomplish in the training session and a way to evaluate whether you've accomplished it.

Before you started the training, you probably asked yourself, "What do I want or need to teach them?" Perhaps you also asked the more important question: "What do I want them to learn?" You should also ask these two key questions:

- How will I know what they've learned? (evidence procedure)
- How should they act after the training?

With many processes, these questions are easy to answer. Either they can do it or they can't. They will improve with practice. But if they're clearly on the right track, that's success.

However, other types of training are more difficult to evaluate. Quality training and sensitivity training fall into this category. Unfortunately, these types of training often fail, not for lack of good intentions but for lack of clear objectives and a way to measure or observe the results of the training.

Any time you plan to train workers, build into your plan a way to follow up. Keep it simple, and tell the learners what will be expected of them: "We'll try this again in a week to see how you do. I hope that you'll all be able to do it with confidence."

Discuss specific performance objectives and timelines. Don't end the training session until everybody knows what's supposed to happen next.

After the training, follow up as promised, especially if you need to send out more materials. Have an evaluation form or survey about the training to help you determine if it was effective (and how to improve).

Training need not be formal, and it shouldn't be frightening for you or for employees.

- Break down the process into manageable sections.
- Get them doing instead of just listening.
- Follow up.

You are the first and best source of on-the-job, on-the-spot training. Do your job well, bring in a coach approach, and watch employees grow in mastery, confidence, and productivity.

The Coach's Checklist for Chapter 8

☑ Before you train others to do a task, make sure you have it mastered yourself.

☑ Bring a coach approach, focused on the *learning*, to your training.

☑ Break down the process you want to teach into steps and keep them simple.

☑ Demonstrate how to do a task, then KYHO (keep your hands off) while the trainee begins to do it.

☑ Set up the training so the trainee experiences a series of small successes leading to the big success of mastery.

☑ Be aware of the four stages of learning: unconscious incompetence, conscious incompetence, conscious competence, and unconscious competence.

☑ Be empathetic with learners, show them respect, and help them build on what they know.

☑ Make sure you have a way to know whether learners have mastered the tasks you're training them in.

The Coach
as Mentor

"Frank," you say, looking him in the eye, "I normally don't give perfect performance evaluations. I've always believed you ought to leave a little room for improvement, even in the best employee. It's a motivator."

Frank looks dubious and a bit wary, waiting for his less-than-perfect work evaluation. "What did I do wrong?" his expression seems to ask.

"In your case," you continue, "I'm going to make an exception. Your work has been fantastic. I can rely on you to do the job right the first time, and you frequently exceed my expectations."

Frank's face flushes, first with surprise, then pleasure. Clearly you've just exceeded his expectations.

"Thank you," he stammers.

"Not at all," you say. "You've earned it. In fact, I think your opportunities for growth in this department are limited. I'd like to help you find a better position in this company, if you like."

Now Frank *really* looks surprised. What kind of manager would work to help his best employees leave his area?

A good coach and mentor, who puts the development of the indi-

MISTAKE PROOFING

LANGUAGE OF THE OFFER

Notice that in this opening example, you *offered* an opportunity ("if you like") of a better position to Frank, rather than *telling him* to apply. Keep your language open and allow the employee to choose. Frank may well be keen on this option, but he might choose another path or counteroffer with something you hadn't thought of. As we've said several times in this book, never make assumptions about other people's wants or needs.

KEY TERM

Mentor A wise, loyal adviser. The word comes from Greek mythology. Mentor was friend and adviser to Odysseus and the teacher of his son, Telemachus.

vidual first, would do just such a thing.

Types of Mentoring

As mentioned in Chapter 2 when we defined coaching, pure coaching is not the same as mentoring. However, just like with training, you *can* bring a coach approach to your role as a mentor with your employees. Blending coaching skills with mentoring creates an even more positive path for your employees and truly demonstrates your focus on them.

There are two kinds of mentoring in business. Both make sense for the mentor, the employee, and the organization. Everybody wins when you mentor effectively.

Mentoring Within the Organization

As a manager, you often must do more than simply train and manage employees. Since you have to look to the bigger picture of the company, you also are responsible for guiding how your employees are a part of that—everything from learning processes and fitting into the corporate culture to career path and development in the organization.

There's more to the job than just the job. Some of the most important stuff never makes it into the personnel manual.

When you walk into the workplace for the first time, you may encounter an invisible web of political intrigue and ancient feuds. Maybe you stepped on a few land mines before you got the lay of the land. Most of the rules aren't written down. The "way we do things here" has evolved with practice and tradition. Folks may not even know why they do things the way they do. Getting up to speed with processes and corporate culture is a key opportunity for mentoring, especially with new hires.

In a larger organization, employees may not be aware of opportunities available to them. Do your best employees know about the Talent Acceleration Program? Do your workers know about the tuition reimbursement benefit if they take graduate-level or certification courses? You are responsible for helping them take advantage of these programs and growing as workers.

Give the people who work with you the benefit of your experience. Mentor them on the things they need to know to flourish within the organization. Be available to answer questions, and support them on their next steps.

Mentoring Beyond the Organization

Mentoring can, of course, extend beyond the workplace. There is often a lot of overlap between any one person's work and life. Employees may come to you for bigger picture mentoring, such as creating work–life balance, goal-setting, and more (possibly even career changing or transitioning to retirement). This means helping individuals chart long-term goals that may not be directly related to their job or the company. Much of that kind of mentoring takes place within the organization. Some people seek mentors who have accomplished the things they themselves want to do, whether that person is inside the company or elsewhere.

Some workers hit a wall, rising as high as they can in a company without going someplace else. Sometimes that wall is you—for example, if you have a couple of workers who are qualified for and want your job, but they can't move forward until you do.

You can try to keep the lid on those employees, hoping through material rewards like merit pay increases and symbolic ones like title changes (or other benefits) to keep them happy enough to stick with you, despite the lack of opportunity to grow.

Or you can help them move up and out, as you did with Frank in the opening example. Keep in mind that "moving up" might mean "moving on" from your company to another opportunity.

Yes, you might lose your organization's best employees that way. You'll have to recruit, hire, and train replacements. It will be a lot of work

MENTORING PERSONAL AND WORK ISSUES

Imagine that Mary comes to you and says she is worried about taking time off for maternity leave, coming up for her in a few months. She is concerned that six weeks off won't be enough, that she'll not perform well when she returns, that she'll be a bad mother if she puts her child in daycare. She is worried about the logistics and costs of child care, nursing, and needing flex time or possibly working from home.

Mary knows that you had a baby three years ago (in this example, you are a working mom) and wonders what your advice would be to her. This is a key example of thinking beyond the organization, and it's a great opportunity for mentoring, blended with a little coaching.

You begin to share your own story with Mary, being honest about the difficulties you encountered and how you handled them, while leaving her free to choose her own path. You also can point out some of the company support available to her. For example, perhaps your company does not have on-site daycare, but they do have a discount deal with a local highly rated preschool and a nanny service. You remind her that a nutritionist comes in twice a month, and this is a great resource for nursing moms, who need more calories and a good diet. You go over the flex time policies with Mary, and brainstorm on how she might be able to do some of her tasks from home in the future.

Mary leaves feeling heard and valued, and she has some great new ideas

for you, with no guarantee that a new person will be as good as the one you lost.

And yet, that's exactly what you should do. Great managers identify, foster, and develop *talent*.

If you don't help employees move upward and onward, you become an adversary or roadblock. They see you as working against their best interests (or even sabotaging them), and that creates tension and distrust, making them more eager to move on. If a constricting economy limits opportunities elsewhere and you "succeed" in keeping that disgruntled employee, you no longer get peak performance, the goal of all coaching.

Effective Mentoring

Effective mentoring can provide four important benefits.

1. Employees view a job with a sense of its possibilities and become more motivated and productive.

2. Employees will be loyal to you (and the company) for as long as they work with you—and when they're working someplace else, too. (It never hurts to have friends and contacts.)

3. Their advancement creates a vibrant working atmosphere, with everyone in the organization working to move up the ladder.

4. You open up jobs in the organization that draw in new blood, new ideas, and new energy.

SUCCESS CULTURE

SMART

MANAGING

Consider the phrase "A rising tide lifts all boats." When you mentor and coach your employees to success, *everyone* succeeds: they do, you do, the department does, the company does. There doesn't need to be winners and losers when *everyone* is winning.

Some workers may not see it that way, and could feel threatened or think you're giving favorable treatment to fast-track certain people to a promotion. Work with these people, too, to ensure everyone's success.

Balance these gains against the time it takes you to recruit and train new workers, and you still come out ahead.

The requirements for being an effective mentor are basic.

- Time
- Energy
- Willingness
- Accurate information
- Caring

We all have time and energy. It's a matter of how we choose to spend them. Once you see how mentoring pays off for you and your company, you'll start to prioritize this important work.

You also need to be *willing* to mentor (and your employees have to be willing to receive it). Do not feel threatened by your employees' success—it reflects well on you. You can demonstrate your willingness to mentor by coaching your employees, supporting them in their goals, and being a resource for them.

You've been gathering information since the day you started working. If you've worked your way up through the ranks, performing the jobs other people now do for you, you know the ins and outs as well as anybody. You know how to get the information you don't already have. Remember, ignorance, your own or anybody else's, is a curable condition. As a manager, you are responsible for imparting that information to your employees, and giving accurate information can be crucial for effective mentoring.

A good mentor (and manager and coach) should truly *care* about his or her employees. If you didn't care about them, why would you even bother mentoring? A good mentor wants everyone to succeed. A coach keeps a client-focused approach, and the mentor should, too. Focus on what your employees want and how you can help them get there. As a manager, you are in the unique position of being able to care about your employees while keeping a big-picture view of the overall goals of the organization.

Everybody has to learn to find his or her own way in the workplace. But you may be able to help your staff past some of the most obvious problems. Let's consider a few key areas to consider in your job as mentor.

Coaching the In-Game

There's the process as it's outlined in the employees' manual, and then there's the way things really work.

Remember the questions you had when you were new to the job. Anticipate the problems a new employee will have. Head off misunderstandings that result in somebody not getting paid for their first month's work or filing for dental insurance after the cut-off date.

THINK LIKE A BEGINNER
Who taught you the lay of the land when you came to your organization? How did you **TOOLS** adjust to the office atmosphere and culture? What do you wish had been in the employee manual? What are the most useful things you learned as you moved up to your managing position? Think like a beginner, and consider the things you need to impart to new hires for them to do well. Ask those around you what *they* would teach new hires, or what they wish they had known when they came aboard.

Who's supposed to sign off on the time sheets? What's the best time to apply for a job reclassification? How detailed do you have to be when you file for expense reimbursement?

The most important element in the in-game stems from the difference between the job description and the actual requirements of the job. Employees need to know what they're really expected to do and how you'll evaluate their work. Mentoring them on these aspects of the work will probably overlap with training.

Taking Emotional Temperatures

Some folks are quite open about expressing how they feel. But many are apt to keep their feelings to themselves, especially when they're new to a job. Don't wait for obvious signs of distress. Inquire after your workers' well-being. Keep it casual, but don't let it become perfunctory.

"How's it going?" isn't fancy, but it's a fine question—if you ask it with genuine concern and a willingness to spend a little time listening to the answer (step up to level 2 or 3 listening; see Chapter 6). Without pushing or prodding, follow up if you suspect a problem: "Are you finding your way around okay?"

Some workers won't

> **AVOID NEGATIVITY**
>
> **CAUTION**
>
> When helping employees learn the in-game, be careful not to make them think that doing one thing but saying another is the norm. Managers in organizations don't always practice what they preach, but avoid saying negative things about other people in the organization that will make those you're mentoring cynical or undermine their enthusiasm to perform well.

respond to what they perceive as being put on the spot. For them, you need to provide safe ways to express feelings and attitudes. The suggestion box (either real or virtual) has become a much belittled cliché, not because it's a bad idea but because the concept has been abused. Too often, employees don't take the process seriously, refusing to offer ideas or coming up with prank suggestions. Employers often ignore suggestions or, worse, retaliate against employees who dare to offer suggestions they don't like.

Consider a variety of methods—including the suggestion box, surveys, bulletin boards, e-mail postings, and open-door office hours—to ensure ample opportunity for employees to express their feelings.

You need this information. You can't coach or mentor without it.

Helping People Move Forward

You might like to think that your staff members want to stay with you forever. And maybe your primary concern is their performance on the job at hand. You want the assistant junior management trainee to devote

100 percent to working at peak performance as an assistant junior management trainee. But she might have her eye on something a little better.

Would you really want a trainee who was content to be a trainee forever? Employees will do their best work for you now out of a strong motivation to move into a better opportunity later. Coach them for as long as you've got them, and help them make realistic career plans. Then do whatever's necessary to support them in making their plans work.

A common question to ask in a job interview is "Where do you see yourself in five years?" This is the kind of thing you should keep in mind and ask your employees about from time to time (great to ask at annual performance reviews). Their goals and desires may change, and you need to keep up with them. If you know that the assistant junior management trainee wants to eventually be a director of a national sales team, you can mentor her on that path as she grows in her role and seeks to move up.

SMART MANAGING

HELP THEM MOVE AHEAD
If you have employees who learn quickly and have talent, think of part of your job as a coach as helping them move ahead. Give them opportunities to shine and take advantage of their talents. It will pay off for them, for you, and for the company.

Take advantage of job evaluation interviews and reviews to conduct formal mentoring. "You've been here three years already, Carol. I suggest you put in for a title change. I can give you the application and walk you through it if you like."

Also look for chances to mentor on the run (or "coachable moments"). Much of your best mentoring will be unscheduled. Be ready to take advantage of opportunities.

Applying the Principles of Basic Humanity

What if you must mentor someone who is older than you? In many cultures, the young defer to the elders, acknowledging the wisdom only experience can teach and only age can confer. The assumption in such cultures is that the old mentor the young. Not so in America, where a 23-year-old manager may supervise a 63-year-old counter worker.

Apply the principles of basic humanity, regardless of age, culture, gender, or any other perceived difference. You have authority over the people who work with you. You will know more than they do in some situations. But remember: You aren't smarter, better, or more important than they are. Treat everyone with respect.

Mentoring to Define the Work

A major part of your job as mentor/manager involves providing accurate, clear information and guidance about work expectations. This goes well beyond providing the job description, as noted, and it also goes beyond clarifying, explaining, and pointing out how the real job differs from the job on paper. In some cases, as industries and markets change, you may be called on to create *new* definitions of work. You should guide workers to positive, creative definitions of their jobs.

Positive Definition of the Work

Somebody has to empty and clean the bedpans in the nursing home. It isn't pleasant, it isn't ego-gratifying, and it isn't well compensated.

You can call it "sanitation engineering" or classify it as a responsibility of the nurses' aides, but don't tie a bow on it. It's still slinging bedpans.

Put the job in the context of the larger goal. Cleaning bedpans is part of creating a healthy, pleasant environment for every resident of the nursing home. It's an important job, and it has positive, worthwhile outcomes.

Creative Definition of the Work

A writer's life used to involve pounding out stories on a manual typewriter (or writing them out longhand). That meant changing a lot of ink ribbons, wadding up a lot of paper, and slathering on a sea of correction fluid. To get an extra copy, the writer had to

> **MISSION STATEMENT**
> Help employees find a connection between their work—even if it seems thankless and menial, like cleaning or emptying bedpans—and the overall mission of the organization (such as "creating a healthy, peaceful environment with the highest standard of care"). With this, you can show the positive impact of even the smallest, most seemingly insignificant task. You don't need to dress up the task in fancy language, but you can draw this connection to the bigger picture.
>
> **TOOLS**

insert a sheet of carbon paper between two sheets of typing paper, put the sandwich into the roller, and type harder.

Now writers type words on a screen and send the work as electronic impulses over the Internet or push a button to print them out from a machine in another room. It's common for books to be written online by writing partners who never meet face to face.

Any writers who defined their job as typing words on paper (the mechanics of the task) locked themselves out of the profession long ago. Those who see their job as conveying information and telling stories (the heart of the job) have adapted to the changing workplace. The tools to get there are different, but the ultimate product remains the same—communication and understanding.

Mentors work to enable employees to define their jobs (and careers) creatively and in terms of a bigger picture—by ultimate purpose, not current tools—so that they will develop the flexibility to adapt and survive. A rigid definition of work won't stand if there's a sudden shift in the industry or the company.

Mentoring to Motivate

You may need to channel the natural motivations people bring with them to the workplace. This kind of mentoring often takes one of two forms: challenging an overachiever or getting an underachiever unstuck. Coaching skills can prove invaluable here!

1. The overachiever. Forget pep talks and lectures. Don't set arbitrary goals or quotas. And definitely don't create busy work. All these approaches simply deepen an overachiever's dissatisfaction and may invite contempt.

CAUTION

WATCH OUT FOR APATHY

Although the core problems are quite different, the symptom is the same: apathy.

An overachiever is bored because there's either not enough to do or nothing to do that provides challenge, stimulates learning, and results in meaningful productivity. The underachiever adopts boredom as a pose to mask insecurity.

One is wading, and the other is drowning. Both want to be swimming with the current, and both feel dissatisfied with their jobs.

You must look beneath the apathy and learn about the worker's abilities to be able to diagnose the problem accurately. Then you can apply the appropriate mentoring and coaching techniques.

Be open and honest, but not confrontational. Share your perception with the worker and discuss possible solutions. Ask for her input. How would she like to be challenged? What skills and talents would she like to put to use? Where does she see opportunity? (These are all terrific coaching questions.) When you can coach her a bit to clarify what she wants, then you bring in some mentorship to get her the resources to do it.

Look for meaningful challenges. Set the bar a little higher, letting the worker succeed one level at a time. Provide additional training opportunities and give increasing amounts of responsibility. Ask the worker to play a leadership role in group settings.

2. The underachiever. Approach an underachiever as an underused resource rather than as a problem to be "fixed." Employees don't want to disappoint you. They're motivated to do good work, and they want to be able to take pride in their work, just as you do.

GETTING MOTIVATED

Jack seems bored. You invite him to your office and ask him about it. He admits he seems a little "checked out" these days, and says clearly that he doesn't feel challenged in his work. He elaborates, with your prompting, and says he feels like he does the same thing every day and only gets to use a limited number of his skills. You learn he's been taking online classes in different programming environments, just to stay sharp.

You ask Jack where he sees some opportunity. He surprises you when he says that he noticed another division in the company sometimes gets bogged down with a mundane computer task that they have to do by hand, which can sometimes take hours. He has learned some scripting tools in one of his classes and feels confident he could create an automatic converter program that would handle the same task in minutes. He decides to work on this side project when he has time at work and at home on the weekends.

Three weeks later, Jack is finished. You arrange a meeting with the other division, where he demonstrates what his program does. You see the jaws drop around the room as the other employees realize what a huge time-saver he has created! Jack's satisfaction is also obvious.

A few months later, you notice that Jack is not only more motivated and driven, but he's identified several other areas where he can start creating solutions. Upper management has noticed—he gets a hefty quarterly bonus for the time he's saved numerous people, and he has several commendation letters. He's also in line for a big promotion with the next budget review.

NO EXCUSES NEEDED

If there's no fault, there's no need for excuses.

You aren't looking for something or someone to blame. You're looking for ways to help a worker do a job better. Be sure to communicate that clearly. With this approach, you'll be working together toward a common goal. The employee will see you as an ally, not a threat.

Pep talks and lectures won't work here, either. Forget carrots and sticks. Again, get the worker involved in a dialogue. They may be afraid to ask for help when they need it. They may not know what resources are available to them. They may be distracted by personal events or other aspects of their lives unrelated to work.

Together, you may be able to create a better match of worker and task. Explore all possibilities, including altering the work environment or routine to get rid of stumbling blocks.

Perhaps a person seems "checked out" and doesn't achieve much because he is distracted by all the tedious meetings, progress reports, gossip, and office politics that goes on. After meeting with him, you offer the opportunity to work from home a couple of days a week, with online availability in case you need to reach him. After a few weeks of trying this revised schedule,

CAUTION

UNDERACHIEVER OR A BAD FIT?

Be aware that an underachiever might just not be right for the job. Despite our best efforts to put the right person in the right job, sometimes it just doesn't work out.

the worker seems more energized at the office, and you notice that he is caught up on all his responsibilities and is doing excellent work.

As with all coaching opportunities, set some guidelines, a way to measure progress, and arrange for a follow-up session.

Respecting the Boundaries of Mentoring

You're a manager, a coach, a mentor. You motivate and guide. You make decisions, evaluate performance, solve problems.

You do not "fix" psychological problems or mediate disputes for one simple reason: You aren't qualified to deal with them. Know your limits!

If you've got a "dysfunctional" department, clearly in need of some group therapy, you've got some alternatives.

- **Bring in an expert.** If your organization is large enough to have an Office of Employee Assistance or a similar department, arrange to have a professional come in, help you establish guidelines, and conduct an extended discussion or series of discussions to work through problems. If you don't have an in-house pro, look to the nearest university extension or outreach program. Many have experts on conflict resolution in the workplace who will work with you for reasonable fees. Hold such sessions away from the workplace, but don't call them "retreats" or half of the workers will hate the process before they ever get started.

- **Create firm boundaries.** If you can't solve the problem, as leader you must enforce a cease-fire. Admit that you can't "fix" things. Don't pretend to be fair. Discuss, develop, and implement guidelines for behavior. Nobody will be happy. They might all blame you. But at least they'll be united in that, and you'll be able to get some work done.

Despite some of the problems and pitfalls inherent in mentoring employees, most of your mentoring will be positive and productive. Combined with training, coaching, and problem solving, it will help move your staff closer to peak performance.

The Coach's Checklist for Chapter 9

☑ There are two types of mentoring: inside the organization and beyond the organization. One teaches skills and organizational savvy; the other helps a person build a career.

☑ To be a successful mentor, you need to have time, energy, willingness, accurate information to share, as well as genuine caring for your employees.

☑ Successful mentors understand that they are no smarter, better, or more important than anyone else. They understand their role as a helper, however, and take it seriously.

☑ Mentors help people understand their work not as tasks but as contributions to a process to deliver an output others will value.

☑ Mentors help bolster employee motivation.

The Coach
as Corrector

Training employees for new procedures, teaching them new skills, and helping them map out a career path are positive roles for a manager/coach.

Correcting inadequate performance and unacceptable behavior in the workplace is more difficult. In this chapter, we discuss some principles that will help you take the sting out of the encounter and make it productive rather than punitive. A coach approach can be helpful in connecting with a worker who needs to improve.

Make It an Encounter, Not a Confrontation

Your attitude going into any correctional situation will largely determine your success or failure. Take a positive, goal-oriented approach (solution-focused). The goal, as always, is better employee performance.

First, focus on the *behavior*, not the person. Avoid talking about a person's tendencies, characteristics, or traits. Focus on specific actions and outcomes and how they need to change.

For example, Jan has been arriving at work 10 to 30 minutes late three or four days a week for several weeks. She doesn't have to punch a time clock, but employees are expected to keep regular hours. Your company frowns on workers taking comp time unless a supervisor approves it in advance.

Rather than send around a memo warning everyone to get to work on time, you decide to call Jan in for some coaching.

No matter what your tone of voice, if you open the discussion with a statement like "You seem to have trouble getting to work on time," it will sound like an accusation (because that's what it is). Jan is apt to react defensively, with a denial, an excuse, or withdrawal. You'll lecture. She'll seethe. You won't accomplish anything positive. The problem is that you focused on Jan, labeling her as chronically late.

Here's how to start the conversation with the focus on the behavior rather than

THEY REACT TO YOU

Before you begin addressing a worker's behavior, recognize your part in the relationship and that the worker may be reacting to your actions to some degree. You may be able to eliminate all or part of the problem by becoming aware of the signals you're giving off through your words and deeds.

Your behavior is easy to change. Check it out first, and see what you can adjust.

DON'T GENERALIZE

If you treat an individual situation as if it was a general problem, you risk causing resentment, rumors, or even an epidemic of ill will.

When you generalize your reaction to everyone, other employees may resent the "troublemaker." If they don't know who the troublemaker is, they may guess at the culprit and spread rumors. They may even decide that there's no advantage in avoiding trouble, because you lump the good and the bad together. By generalizing your correction, you may be increasing the problem you're trying to resolve.

the person: "I've noticed that you've been getting to work a bit late."

Jan might still react defensively, but you have a better basis for discussion, especially if you make it clear that you're looking for solutions: "Is there anything we can do about that?"

Second, focus on the specific, not the general. Avoid absolutes, like "always" and "never," as in "You're always late" or "You're never on time." When using these absolutes, you've made a sweeping generalization—

which simply turns the truth into an exaggeration, a lie. Since it's an exaggeration, it's impossible to prove—and foolish to try.

You'll back down from a generalization if you're wise. But you might start quibbling about small points to make some sort of case. Even if you win the debate, you'll lose ground in your relationship with Jan. You may succeed in getting her to arrive at work on time, but it may be a hollow victory.

Specific is better. Present your observation to Jan, giving her detailed information about the problem as you see it: "You've been getting to work anywhere from 10 to 30 minutes late three or four days a week." If you start like that, you'll be talking about specific behaviors rather than generalizations or character traits.

Now you can bring in a coach approach. Has Jan been punctual before now? If so, you might want to ask what is going on in her life to make this sudden change. You might have to step into your role as mentor to remind her of corporate policies regarding comp time and working hours, and point out that the meeting is not about punishing her but about finding solutions. Connect with her to find out her thoughts about how she can correct the behavior.

You're a coach, not a cop. You're seeking performance, not punishment or judgment. You need to do what *works*, not what feels good.

Positive Specific Action

Aim for change, not blame. Don't simply tell an employee what not to do. Coach toward positive behaviors. What is the employee supposed to do? What might the impact of correct behavior be? How can the employee get there?

The way you describe the problem (character flaw, chronic condition, or specific behavior) is crucial. After you've defined the behavior, you want to talk about it as specifically as you can, following up with these two steps to create a positive specific action (PSA).

Step 1. Identify why the behavior needs changing. This might seem obvious to you. You assume employees know why they shouldn't arrive late for work, for example. But assumptions seldom make for effective communication. In all but the most obvious situations, you need to be clear and specific as to why the behavior needs changing. Connect it to the big picture of the business and the employee's role in the company. Ask the employee to describe it as well.

Aside from the fact that Jan's lateness cheats the system and angers her coworkers—who are looking to you to be fair—how does it affect the quality of work (hers and others')? The more specific you are here, the more likely it is that Jan will buy into your viewpoint and change her behavior.

Again, keep it positive—focus more on what results the solution would bring than on why the behavior is unacceptable.

Step 2. Ask a question that points toward a solution. Such a question can take many forms, depending on several factors—the problem, the situation, and your relationship with the employee. In some instances, you might simply shrug your shoulders or raise an eyebrow, waiting for the other person to step in with his or her own solutions.

> ### PREPARE YOUR REASONING
>
> Prepare your reasoning before you meet with the employee.
>
> First, write down your reasons for wanting to correct the behavior. Then, try to look at each reason from other points of view. What seems logical or reasonable or necessary from your perspective may not seem so to the employee.
>
> If your list of reasons gets reduced to something like "because it's company policy" or "because that's how I like to run my department," you may want to think about the situation a little more before you meet with the employee. Is it really their problem or yours?

What might most effectively open up a discussion of possible solutions? Who should be responsible for suggesting solutions? You may choose to put the burden

- on the employee ("What can you do to improve?"),
- on both of you ("How can we work together to improve this?"), or
- on the process ("What happens next?").

In many cases, the *process* approach yields the best results. Don't discount the other approaches though—showing your support and empowering the employee with responsibility can also be effective. In fact, you may co-create a hybrid approach that uses elements of all three.

Asking questions that focus on the solution will lead you and the employee to some sort of action plan. For instance, you ask Jan what's going on in her life and find out that her children, who go to a year-round school, have been on their break at home for the past three weeks, and because they aren't on a regular schedule and make demands of her, she finds it difficult to leave on time each morning. From this, you know that when her kids are in school, Jan will likely be more punctual, but on a semi-regular basis, she may have difficulty arriving at her assigned time for a few weeks.

You use a process approach and ask Jan what should be done next. She tosses out a few options and asks about schedule shifting. She proposes coming in an hour later than usual and staying an hour later than usual, just for those weeks when her kids aren't in school. This leads to your needing to check with HR and other managers to find out if it's acceptable (your responsibility). Together, you also come up with a backup plan in case that doesn't work: Jan will work some extra hours to earn comp time during her regular weeks, and then let you and her colleagues know that she'll be in an hour later in some weeks (preapproval of comp time; her responsibility).

Awareness of the PSA will force you to think before you coach, and that will make you a better coach.

Define Consequences Clearly

You need to be clear about what's at stake. The trickiest part of any attempt to change someone's behavior comes when you confront the "or else?" question. Whether or not the employee asks, you need to be very clear about the consequences. As a manager, you have to enforce the consequences from time to time. You may not like it, but that's the price of authority.

First, be specific. Vague mumblings to "shape up or ship out" or warnings that "we could have a bigger problem" accomplish nothing—except making you look ineffectual. High-sounding language about "dire repercussions and sanctions" is no better—just more pompous. State potential consequences specifically.

Second, avoid a threatening tone. Your goal is to change the behavior, not punish the employee. Make sure your tone as well as your words convey your focus on this goal. Soften your expression, keep a warm note in your voice, and relax your body language.

Finally, never invoke a consequence that won't happen. We all learned a long time ago to disregard phony warnings and other empty threats.

You should have specific procedures in place for dealing with inadequate performance and unacceptable workplace behavior. Your company may have guidelines on this to some extent (i.e., written reprimands, docking pay, etc.), but you also may be responsible for creating your own system of correcting behavior.

ACTIONS AND CONSEQUENCES

As much as possible, the consequences you cite should arise naturally from the actions, rather than being imposed. It's better to talk about your concern that the team might not complete certain tasks or meet its performance goals or reach its objectives, rather than about sanctions such as docked pay.

TOOLS

If you can't come up with any specific consequences in terms of performance, consider that you might be dealing with a behavior you'd be better off overlooking (if it's minor). Again, that decision depends on the employee and your relationship with him or her. You may be able to correct behavior simply by showing concern or by making some adjustments.

Company procedures outline sequential steps, typically moving from verbal warning through written reprimand to a letter in the personnel file. Further problems may result in suspension, demotion, and, ultimately, termination.

You need to know the organization's procedures and your authority within them—that's your role as a manager. Failure to follow the procedures is unfair and, in some cases, illegal.

So don't say it unless you're prepared to back it up. If you don't follow through, your words won't have much influence the next time or with other employees.

Build on the Possible

Is it really a behavior problem? You may be assuming that the employee *won't*. Consider the possibility that she or he *can't*—but doesn't want you to know it.

Take me, for example, coach. No matter how many times you tell me, no matter how often you show me, and no matter how much you threaten punishment if I fail, or promise rewards if I succeed, I'm not going to be able to dunk a basketball (except in my dreams, of course). I'm a little too short and don't have a great vertical leap.

Can't you let me do something else, instead? I'm a good point guard because I can see who's free to make a basket, I'm great at stealing the ball from the opponent, and I can nail deadly accurate passes to my teammates.

Start with what an employee *can* do and work toward what she or he isn't doing yet. Begin formal and informal performance evaluations with strengths, not weaknesses. Whenever possible, emphasize those strengths by allowing employees to do more of what they do well, leading them by steps into increasingly difficult and more complex tasks. Then build on those strengths to help the worker succeed in new areas.

Sometimes folks work better in teams, even as each performs a solo task. If you partner a struggling worker with a confident, capable one, you may help the first worker improve performance. You also help the capable worker grow his or her skills as a mentor and teacher. Everyone wins.

You may recognize the benefits of natural cross-training here. Employees who work as partners or in teams tend to know more about what the other teammates are doing. That makes it easier if you need to shift responsibilities when somebody is absent or if job demands suddenly change.

Remember: One size does not fit all, and a single formula for measuring productivity can't adequately measure every worker's performance. Your goal must be to bring each employee to his or her peak level of performance (or as close to it as possible)—not to an arbitrary performance standard for all employees (not to mention standards for other areas of behavior).

Even if compensation is based on an absolute scale—as when an employee is paid per project completed or unit sold—you must evaluate each person by an individual and subjective scale. Treating all employees fairly and acknowledging what's possible for them to achieve *doesn't* mean treating them all the same.

Look to the Future

You want results, not excuses. What counts is what the employee does next.

Be clear about how past performance or behavior has failed to meet expectations. But once you've done this, move on to specific goals and a future framework. Let the past go. Don't hold grudges (in your head or in the employee's personnel folder). Give employees the chance to make it right and get beyond the problem.

A good coach is always future-focused. You can bring this viewpoint to the employee. Learn from the past—what worked, what didn't—and then turn toward creating a positive future. Sometimes this takes practice, especially when you're trying to define what you want in a positive way.

Don't Go Worst Case

SMART MANAGING

When you describe behavior that needs changing, it's easy to go to a worst-case scenario, pointing out all the bad things that can happen. "Susan, if you don't stop calling these unnecessary meetings, productivity will slip, profits will go down, your team will resent you, you'll get demoted and eventually fired."

Obviously, as a manager, you do have to state the negative side effects of behavior that needs changing. But remember to counter with the best-case scenario of what happens when the person changes. "If you can cut your scheduled meetings in half, the whole department will have more time to work on their projects, producing more, earning more, and getting you a promotion!" (Granted, that might be an exaggeration, but you get the picture.)

Once you've described the behavior that needs changing, be sure to focus on what you *do want* to happen in the future. It's easy to say, "Well, we don't want this office gossip to continue!" In those cases, you (and the employee) are still focused on what you *don't want*. Remember to turn it around to what you do want in the future. "If we have less office gossip, we are creating a peaceful, supportive environment for everyone to work in." This offers a positive image to work toward.

Performance Killers

Here are some correction methods that will guarantee failure in any attempts to correct poor performance or unacceptable behavior in employees. For discussion purposes, we group these methods under three general headings: false judgment, false solution, and avoidance.

False Judgment

- Diagnosing
- Psychoanalyzing
- Labeling/stereotyping
- Nonspecific praising/supporting

There's a big difference between judging the behavior or performance of a worker and judging the worker as a person.

Avoid diagnosing ("Your problem is that you have a bad attitude") and psychoanalyzing ("You've got a problem accepting a male authority figure because your father died when you were 11"). You don't have the necessary training or enough information to make such characterizations. They'll just get in your way as you try to deal with an employee. And many will take offense when you make such a statement. You have essentially dismissed their viewpoint by slapping a label on them.

You would never consider applying a racial, ethnic, or gender stereotype to a worker. (Unfortunately, we're all only too familiar with prejudices.) But watch out for more subtle stereotypes (the way "those people" think or behave). Any conclusion based on a categorical generalization, such as age, educational background, clothing, or anything else, erodes your ability to manage and coach.

ASSUME WITH CARE
All managers understand the need to be sensitive to differences among employees, right? Sometimes those differences are easier to notice because of race, ethnicity, or gender, right?

You may start to slip into a dangerous area here. You should be *sensitive* to differences but should avoid *assuming* differences. Especially be careful to avoid assuming that anything that makes an individual different will necessarily affect that person's behavior or performance.

Even such positive reinforcement as praise or a compliment can make you a less effective coach if it's based on generalizations. The statement "You've got an MBA, so you must really know your stuff" is just as likely to be inaccurate as "You're doing well for a woman." Be careful that your praise doesn't convey a feeling of surprise, as if you had lower expectations for an employee: "Wow! Great job tightening that bolt!" might be taken as meaning "You've got a scraggly beard and long hair and an earring, so I was wondering what kind of work we could get out of you." Sometimes it is just a subtle matter of not praising excessively.

False Solution

- Cracker barrel philosophy
- Morality tales
- Unsolicited advice

"To thine own self be true," Polonius advises Laertes in *Hamlet*. "And it follows as the night the day, you must be true to all men."

Sage advice from a wise elder? Then why did audiences at the old Globe Theatre snicker when they heard those words?

Folks in Shakespeare's day called such windy pontifications "copy book wisdom," because school children copied the phrases to practice penmanship. The advice is good—it's just tired and not all that helpful.

Even if your words of wisdom came from your parents rather than Shakespeare, workers may not want or need to hear them.

That's true whether you're quoting Shakespeare, telling

> ### OPINIONS MATTER
> Voicing a negative judgment may bring swift, negative reaction. Just holding the negative opinion, even if you never state or overtly act on it, hurts you as a manager. Your false assumptions automatically make you less aware of a worker's abilities and muddle your ability to make decisions.
>
> It's still a free country and you have a right to your opinions. But on the job you're responsible for being a good manager. What good manager underestimates assets and undermines decision making?

the tale of the ant and the grasshopper, or sharing an experience from your past. Don't assume that employees will be interested in your story or find it helpful. Platitudes like "slow and steady wins the race" are worn out and tired. Think about your sage words, your tales of wisdom, and the lessons you've learned along life's path. If you truly believe that something will help employees develop, share it. If not, save it for a more appropriate occasion.

ABC

TOOLS

One of the most helpful coaching principles you can apply is ABC: Ask before coaching. (This applies to giving advice, too.) Sometimes a person complains just to blow off steam, and they don't really want advice or your thoughts. Never jump in with unsolicited advice or coaching to someone—they may see you as trying to "fix" them, when all they really wanted was a sympathetic ear. If you ask them if they want your opinion, advice, or some coaching, some will say yes, and some won't.

That brings us to the final performance killer in this section: unsolicited advice.

If you find yourself starting a sentence with "This is really none of my business," your next words should not be "but if you ask me . . . " Try saying, "so I'll keep my mouth shut" instead. Then do it. If that employee is curious, she'll ask. (Be careful to avoid intimidating her into asking.)

Avoidance

- Diversion
- The old bob and weave
- Later
- False assurance

Refusing to deal with an issue may buy you a little time, but it also may make the situation worse. The longer you allow poor performance or unacceptable behavior to continue, the more reinforced and established that behavior becomes. Your silence sends employees the message that you approve of the behavior or at least accept it.

The employees who are guilty of the poor performance or unacceptable behavior then feel free to continue, and others might let their performance slide or worry less about their behavior. Your problem just grows. You may be seen as a weak manager for avoiding tackling the issue head on.

Don't keep changing the subject. Diversion and avoidance are not solutions. Deal with it.

Another classic avoidance technique is "the old bob and weave." We invite you to watch a performance by experts (a veteran TV reporter trying to pin down an equally veteran politician).

As we join the program already in progress, the reporter wants to confirm rumors (based on "usually reliable" but unnamed sources, of course) that the politician has racially harassed a campaign worker. Knowing that any reply on the subject will hurt him, the politician attempts to divert by seeming to take the high ground.

Reporter (looking concerned and serious): Sir, how would you respond to the disturbing reports regarding your racial harassment during the recent campaign?

Politician (smiling broadly and nodding): I appreciate your question. But you know, the real issue facing the American people (turning a sincere gaze to the camera) is the lack of adequate health care protection for over 40 percent of working Americans today. Now, the bill I have just placed before Congress . . .

This dance can go on forever. The reporter talks about racial slurs and insults, and the politician talks about his push for appropriations.

The next avoidance technique on the list is "later," as in "never, if I'm lucky." Managers often slip out from under a problem by thinking, like Scarlett O'Hara in the classic tale *Gone With the Wind*, "Tomorrow's another day."

You really should talk to Geoff about his poor performance, but you dread the task. You have a lot of "real" work to do, after all, and surely another day won't hurt.

But another day will hurt. Tomorrow turns into today, and you're even less willing and able to face the difficult confrontation. Time may heal all wounds, but it doesn't solve most performance and behavior problems in the workplace. They won't usually be "gone with the wind."

False assurance can be as harmful as any other form of avoidance. "Nothing to worry about," you tell the worker grandly. "This will work itself out." The worker leaves feeling better—or not, depending on how much trust you've earned—while the problem continues to grow.

Don't let any of these performance killers get in your way. They're all evasions of your responsibility to confront poor performance.

Workers are responsible for the consequences of their actions. But as a supervisor, you're responsible (and accountable) for managing their performance. Even if they're at fault, you must take responsibility for improving the situation.

As manager, you must be coach, problem solver, trainer, teacher, mentor, and corrector. Prepare for all these roles, and approach each with a positive, goal-oriented attitude. No matter what hat you wear, or how many you wear at one time, your ultimate goal must always be the same: helping workers achieve peak performance.

No matter how firm your resolve to accept this responsibility and tackle problems head on, some basic characteristics of the human beings you work with might get in your way as you attempt to become an effective coach. We discuss those potential pitfalls—and solutions to them—in the next chapter.

The Coach's Checklist for Chapter 10

- ☑ When you're correcting employees, remember to make it an encounter, not a confrontation.
- ☑ Avoid accusing the employee; examine the specific behaviors and try to understand them and their causes together.
- ☑ Use positive specific action (PSA) to help employees improve behavior. This includes defining the behavior and why it needs to change, asking questions that lead to a solution, and then agreeing on that solution.
- ☑ If change doesn't happen, let the employee know the specific consequences.
- ☑ Make sure the employees have the capabilities to do what's asked. Don't assume they do without checking on that.
- ☑ Once you've dealt with the problem, let the past go and look to the future—that's better for the coach and the employee.
- ☑ Performance killers include making false judgments, providing false solutions, and avoiding the problem.

Coaching Trouble Spots

G ood intentions and skills alone won't make you a good coach. Even applying all the great advice from the first 10 chapters of this book aren't enough to get the job done if you fall into any of the potential pitfalls we discuss in this chapter.

These coaching land mines can be hard to spot, but once you locate them they're easy to avoid.

Lack of Authentic Purpose

A dog often circles—sometimes several times—before settling down to sleep. The most popular explanation is that this is a defensive behavior left over from wilderness days. The dog circles to get a 360° look at the surroundings to make sure no enemies are near. The fact that dogs sense the presence of other creatures primarily through smell, not sight, seems to weaken the theory.

Basically, dogs circle because that's what dogs do. Dogs circle, owls hoot, and washing your car seems to make it rain. It's just the way things are.

KNOW WHEN TO TRY SOMETHING ELSE

Some of the trouble spots in this chapter simply won't respond to coaching, no matter how good a coach you are. Remember: You *can't* change another person. The other person has to *want* to change and be willing to do so. Trying to coach someone who has no desire to change is a waste of time. Know when you have to abandon coaching and try another technique.

You and your workers may be doing a bit of circling around before you settle down in the workplace, too. Rituals can be important, such as getting that first cup of coffee and sipping it while processing e-mail, before getting to the meat of the work day. Although this kind of habit might not be strictly productive, it may allow a person's brain to "wake up" and get focused. Habits such as a daily "walkabout" to casually chat with co-workers might not serve much purpose and may hinder productivity.

When you first study the principles of time management, you may be amazed at how often you'll catch yourself doing things that have no clear benefit to you or anybody else, simply because you did them the day before, and the day before that, and the day before. A time audit can be quite enlightening!

TRICKS OF THE TRADE — TIME AUDIT

Every now and then, do an audit of how you spend your time. Keep a detailed log for a few days to see how much time you spend on what tasks. Then categorize those tasks by purpose (and payoff). You might be surprised with how much time you spend doing things that seem like "busy-work," or even how much time gets wasted in nonproductive activities.

Note that it's not possible to totally eliminate time wasters. Not every second in the day can be 100 percent productive! But a time audit will give you an idea of where you can focus your efforts. Teach your employees this technique as well.

Make sure your management behaviors don't fall into that category. Have a purpose for everything you do. Remind yourself not only of what you should do but of what you hope to accomplish by doing it.

Here are three ways to avoid performing purposeless activities.

1. Don't just do it to be doing it. People do certain things because they've always done them. They do them because the person who had the job before them did those things. They do them because someone told them to (or they read it in a book). They do them so that someone will see them. They do them so that they can say they did them.

These are not strong or compelling reasons to do anything. Look for the real reason behind the practice—and abandon it if it doesn't serve a useful purpose.

CALENDAR REVIEW

Dana had read a great book on time management skills two years ago. She tried a technique from the book that involved reviewing her calendar for five minutes at the end of each workday. She noted upcoming meetings and appointments, other deadlines and responsibilities, and shifted anything that needed changing. On Thursdays, she would review the following week's calendar for a few extra minutes. And once a month, she sat down and did some long-range planning and review of her calendar.

When Dana's manager challenged her to examine her tasks and find her time wasters, she thought about her calendar review and why she was doing it. Sure, she had read it in a business book and tried it out. When she examined the results from this habit, she realized that she had a greater purpose for keeping up with it: It gave her a sense of control about her time and tasks, which considerably lowered her stress and sense of feeling frazzled. She noticed that in the two years she had been practicing this habit, she hadn't missed any deadlines, so her productivity had increased. In fact, she was able to take on a bit *more* work because she could pace herself better, and she had gotten a title promotion because of it.

In Dana's case, the calendar review may have started as a tip to act on, but it helped her create a more positive environment, something she wanted more of.

---

2. Don't mistake the activity for the results. Does the rooster really believe that his wild crowing makes the sun rise?

When people link cause and effect erroneously (as when the baseball player refuses to wash his lucky socks during a hitting streak), it's called superstition. In the workplace, it's called a waste of time. But people don't always spot erroneous cause-and-effect links. So they go on mistaking an activity (such as reading a document) with the desired result (making sense of the words on the page), resulting in the assertion "Yeah, I read it, but I didn't understand it."

The goal is peak performance. If quality circles or mastermind groups help employees perform better, then have them. But quality circles—and meetings, committees, reports, memos, phone calls, and training sessions—must not become an end in themselves.

It's easy to be seduced by hot business trends, tools, and buzzwords—tiger teams, TQM, Six Sigma, and so on. It's natural to want to jump on the bandwagon, keep up with the competition, ride the cutting edge by establishing what's new and hot right now. Be sure any new initiative has a clear purpose and goal behind it. They must be the means to some clear goal. If the activity doesn't get you the result you want, do something else.

3. Keep it relevant. Most people would rather be busy than bored or active rather than idle. It feels good to produce, especially when the output is tangible.

Writers feel a sense of well-being as the computer screen fills with words. But they don't get paid strictly for filling screens with words; they get paid for writing something that other people want or need to read. That involves thinking, and sometimes the thinking requires that they stop "making progress" at the computer screen and instead spend some time staring, pacing, and muttering.

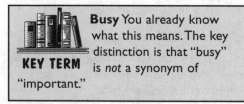

Busy You already know what this means. The key distinction is that "busy" is *not* a synonym of "important."

KEY TERM

Don't mistake *motion* for *progress*. You may be making great time, but if you're heading in the wrong direction, your speed is only taking you further from your goal.

How often do you hear the following dialogues?

Dialogue 1

John: Hey, boss! Have you got a minute?

Mary: Not now. I'm busy.

Dialogue 2

Bill: Hey, Mary. Have you got a minute?

Mary: Of course!

These conversations occurred within 30 seconds of each other. Mary was busy one moment, then the next moment she could spare some time. What was the difference? Simple: position. John works for Mary, and Mary works for Bill. Mary was too busy for John, but not too busy for Bill.

Take your "work pulse" from time to time. Are you using "busy" as if it really means "important"? Remember: it's good to be busy with important things, but it's bad to be busy doing things to be important.

Anxiety (Yours)

No one likes to admit it, but most people experience some level of anxiety in their day-to-day dealings with others. The anxiety can become especially acute when they must deliver bad news, correct unacceptable behavior, improve inadequate performance, or many of the other tasks that can burden a manager.

Anxiety is natural and unavoidable. It can even be helpful if you focus and channel the anxiety as energy available to help you do the job. Think of being "keyed up" instead of nervous or scared.

The first step in dealing with anxiety, then, is to admit you're feeling it. Then decide if you can harness that energy or if you need to work on reducing it (a good moment for self-coaching).

Nothing combats anxiety better than preparation. Some managers choose to prepare obsessively, making sure that everything is planned carefully, down to the last detail. But sometimes you just don't have that much time to prepare. Sometimes all that preparation can hurt you if you encounter something unexpected—such as an unusual question, a mechanical glitch, or a last-minute schedule change.

What if you can't prepare? How do you deal with anxiety then?

Here's a little lesson from Linus in the comic strip *Peanuts*. He deals with the anxieties of his world by carrying around a security blanket. Whatever happens, he can fight his anxiety by holding his blanket close.

What works for Linus might work for you, in a more metaphorical sense. You might keep something in your pocket that will give you a lift, inspire you, remind you of what really matters to you. It could be a picture of someone you love, a lucky penny, a pebble that reminds you of a vacation by the sea, or the keys to your Porsche.

BACK OF THE BUSINESS CARD

Whatever the cause of your anxiety, you can often apply the back-of-the-business-card technique to get ready to tackle it.

Take a business card, turn it over, and write three key words or phrases that outline the steps you need to take or the points you need to make in a conversation. Save a little space to note *when* you'll take these steps.

If you can do this in advance of a stressful situation, carry the card around with you so that you can take it out and glance at it whenever the anxiety returns. As the moment approaches, allow yourself one more "rehearsal" by reviewing your points.

This technique works even when you have only a couple of minutes to prepare. It will ease your anxiety and improve your performance.

What do you miss most when you're at work? What keeps you grounded or makes you feel most at ease when you leave the office? Carrying a piece of that good feeling as a totem or touchstone may help you through your times of anxiety.

Fear/Distrust (Theirs)

Employees may be afraid of you or distrust you simply because you're the boss. It's nothing personal, but if you sit in the boss's chair, behind the boss's desk, you may evoke those feelings. Even if you used to work side by side with them, when you're promoted, you are then seen in a different light.

Although that's not your fault, you need to take responsibility for managing their fear and distrust.

Fear may wear many disguises. It may cause employees to react defensively, be excessively deferential, frequently make excuses, or avoid you. On the theory that the best defense is a strong offense, some employees may challenge your authority in various ways, acting out their fear aggressively.

Many frightened people adopt an unconscious strategy called passive resistance. When you coach, manage, or mentor them, they nod pleasantly and mumble agreement. They just don't do what you told them to do, because they're afraid to displease you by doing it wrong. They're only giving you lip service and aren't really invested.

Once you become aware that fear is motivating any employee, you can begin to combat that fear.

The first step is to acknowledge that you might be doing something to create or nurture the fear. Examine your own behaviors for anything that might appear threatening, even though you don't intend it

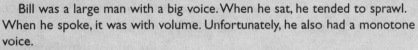

BE AWARE OF YOURSELF!

FOR EXAMPLE

Bill was the president of a small company. He tried hard to be friendly toward all his employees, but he was unaware that he was constantly undermining those efforts.

Bill was a large man with a big voice. When he sat, he tended to sprawl. When he spoke, it was with volume. Unfortunately, he also had a monotone voice.

When he met with employees or managers, he didn't realize that some of them felt intimidated, as much by those aspects of his physical presence as by his position as president. If he made a statement, they felt he was laying down the law. If he asked a few questions, they felt that he was giving them the third degree. Even his casual attitude, which should have been an asset, worked against him—his informality was interpreted as a lack of respect.

What was Bill doing to inspire fear? Nothing but being himself. But he was guilty of not being self-aware—and many people suffered, including Bill.

that way.

Once you've mitigated potentially threatening behaviors, work quietly to overcome employee fear by offering genuine assurance. Something as simple as a smile can be enormously helpful here.

(Of course, it should be clear that you shouldn't do anything to punish a fearful employee. Don't say anything about it. No matter how kind your intentions, making a reassuring comment such as

IT'S NOT ALL YOUR FAULT

CAUTION

Behavior you identify as passive resistance may stem from fear, but you may not be the source of that fear. Employees come to the job not only with fears but personal hostilities and idiosyncrasies. Some of their feelings may relate to you and your behaviors and you may be able to address them, but others have nothing to do with you and, if they don't affect employee performance, are none of your business.

"Well, now, I hope you're not so scared of me anymore" punishes the employee.)

Resistance to Change

Most people resist change—in their routines and patterns, the way they think, and the assumptions they hold. The familiar is comfortable, the unknown is scary. Even if the status quo isn't great, at least it's the "devil you know."

Here's a quick exercise to demonstrate how comfortable we get with even simple habits. Fold your arms across your chest. Now unfold them, and put the "bottom" arm on top. Most people, when they do this, feel weird and uncomfortable. It feels unnatural to have your arms the opposite from how they normally would be. It takes thought and intention to change them.

It Isn't Personal

Don't take resistance to change personally.

If you're initiating changes, it's natural to think the resistance is a reaction to you. But remember that it's the *changes* they're resisting, not you or your authority. Work through the changes together, stressing your common goals and the reasons the changes will help all of you reach those goals.

The same thing will happen if you take the "wrong" shoe off first when you undress tonight or brush your teeth with your nondominant hand. People are creatures of habit, and anything other than the habitual way of doing things can feel downright weird.

When you coach an employee toward peak performance, you may challenge well-established habits and thought patterns. When you adopt new coaching strategies, you disrupt your own sense of well-being and balance.

First acknowledge this resistance in yourself and others. Look past the initial unwillingness to try, the automatic "no." Be patient, with yourself and with others. Acknowledge and allow for backsliding. The moment you stop concentrating on what you're doing, you'll revert to old patterns. Give yourself and employees time to establish new patterns. True growth happens when we push beyond our comfort zone a bit (or a lot).

A MONTH TO A NEW HABIT

SMART

MANAGING

Research into habit-forming and neurological patterns (Maxwell Maltz, *Psycho-Cybernetics*, 1989) found that it takes at least 21 days for a person to form a new habit. The circuits in the brain must be "bombarded" for 21 days in a row with the new data, behavior, or activity to create a lasting habit. During those three weeks, it takes effort and intention to stick with the new habit. After that time, it's "background"—it's automatic.

When creating a change—either in yourself or with your employees—give it a consistent effort for long enough! Don't give up after a week. And if you're trying to shepherd a change in a group of people, you'll probably need longer than three weeks.

Lack of Coaching Skills

Think of something you do well. Perhaps you're a better than average bridge player, possess a dangerous backhand on the tennis court, can whip up a mean stir fry, or have the touch to lay a dry fly just upstream from a feeding trout. You weren't born with these skills. You had to first learn and then develop them.

You weren't born with all the skills you need to be an effective coach, either. Some of the behaviors might not come naturally to you. Acknowledge and work on (or around) your weaknesses. It's just as important to celebrate your strengths and build on them. Note your progress as you continue to become a better coach. Support yourself by reading coaching books, attending training seminars or online classes, and getting mentorship from another coach if you can.

Workers may lack the skills they need to receive coaching effectively. They may have never experienced a manager who discusses problems and procedures with them and values their input. They may not know how to participate in problem solving. They may not be used to looking at their roles in the big picture of the business and industry. They might have difficulty tapping their own resources and potential because no one has ever challenged them to do so.

Don't assume that either you or any particular worker will take to this procedure naturally. You both might have to work at it. That will help, not hinder, the process—as long as you work together.

> **GHOSTS OF TEACHERS PAST**
>
> **CAUTION**
>
> Most of us have known some bad teachers or at least had some bad experiences with teachers. Over the years, we've left them behind—or so we believe. But memories of them can interfere with how we learn later in life.
>
> Perhaps the worst-case scenario is that of an employee who once had a terrible teacher, somebody who made him feel stupid, and he disliked school from then on. Now, years out of school, he still has trouble learning, because he's nagged by those memories and the self-doubt from years past. He might not be fully conscious of the effects of that bad teacher or be able to express them, but he feels them.
>
> What can you do? Be sensitive, be caring, be the best coach you can be, but don't be surprised if you encounter image problems.

Explain what you're doing and why. Admit your own uncertainties about the changes. Then learn the processes together.

Language Barriers

Aquí se habla coaching? If you speak only English, and your employee speaks only Spanish, you know you've got a communication problem, and you must work to solve it. That may not be easy, but at least you recognize the communication barrier.

But what about the *invisible* language barrier? That happens when you both think you're speaking the same language, but you're not communicating. You may have a problem and not even realize it.

Two types of language barriers can block effective communication between you and an employee—jargon and assumption.

The Jargon Barrier

If your third base coach ordered you to put down a suicide squeeze, would you know what you were supposed to do?

You would if you understood baseball jargon. You're being instructed to bunt the next pitch, preferably hard enough to get it past the charging first and third basemen. The runner at third will be breaking for the plate as soon as the pitcher releases the ball. If you don't make contact with the ball, he'll be an easy out. But you can't hit it hard enough that the charging infielders have a play at home. Got it now?

Each sport has its own jargon. So do all industries, hobbies, and professions. Most of us wouldn't know a butterfly stitch from a Butterball turkey, but any good medical intern knows what it is and how to tie one.

Managers develop jargon (including buzzwords), too, and then forget that the rest of the world doesn't understand their language—and may have no interest in learning it. Don't bury your workers in phrases from your last management seminar unless you're willing and able to translate and unless they have some need to know the terminology. If not, stick with a language you both understand.

Employees who don't understand your language may not say anything to you about it. They don't want to appear "dumb," so they are likely to just nod and smile, as if they get it. They could also feel that if you use too much jargon or too many buzzwords that you're just talking to talk and you don't really mean anything by it, again discounting what you're trying to say.

Don't let your words get in the way of your intentions.

The Assumption Barrier

People use language just as they use money. They exchange words and they exchange currency, trusting in a shared understanding of the value of both words and money. After all, a dollar is a dollar, right? Not always.

What would you do for a dollar? Probably not much; it's just change to you. But to an eight-year-old, it might mean a treat from the candy store.

How about $10,000? Now you're interested! But would it interest Bill Gates, Donald Trump, and Ted Turner? For them, it might not even buy a decent suit.

Similarly, everyone knows the face value of words (more or less), but individuals tend to have different values for many words.

Take *ASAP*, for example. Most folks can tell you that "ASAP" stands for "as soon as possible" and that it means "do it right away." But if you tell an employee to get the job done ASAP, you may mean "within the next five minutes" or "before I get back from lunch," but the employee may think you mean "as soon as you get done with what you're working on now" or "before you go home this afternoon."

Such common coinage can be dangerous because both sender and receiver assume they know what it means. Only later do they discover that their assumptions didn't match.

If you need it done before lunch, say so. Be very clear and recheck as necessary.

Coaching Obstacles

Under the category of obstacles, we take on a handful of some of the more minor but still troublesome trouble spots you may find along the road to effective coaching.

The One-Way Street

If you're doing all the communicating, you may not be communicating at all.

Written communication and voice-mail messages carry an obvious danger: Without feedback from the receivers, you have no way of knowing if they've gotten (let alone understood) what you said. If they don't respond, you might think that they don't like what you said or that they don't agree with it. If you react to that assumption, you could really mess things up.

LOOK WHO'S TALKING

CAUTION

Professional coaches don't do much talking during a coaching session. Instead, they ask powerful questions and let the client do most of the talking. Do a quick check: When you are coaching your employees, who's doing most of the talking? If it's you, then you may not be really coaching—you might be telling, teaching, giving advice, or mentoring. All of these are appropriate in your role as manager. When you can add in the coach approach, you'll be doing a *lot* more listening and inviting the employee to offer his or her unique talents to the conversation. This deepens the meaning of any mentoring, managing, and teaching that you might offer.

Even face-to-face communication can be deceptive. Workers may appear to listen attentively, even nod in seeming comprehension, smile, and say "Yep" at all the right places—and still have no idea what you're talking about.

Why don't they just ask? Perhaps because they don't want to look stupid in your eyes. As children, we all learned to bluff in school, where looking confused can draw the teacher's fire.

Ask for questions and, of course, be open to them. But you must do more. Rather than passively waiting for the listener to indicate a lack of understanding, provide specific information and then actively seek confirmation of understanding. For example, when you finish a series of complicated instructions, follow them up with "Now, tell me what you're going to do."

The Interrogation

When a homicide detective on TV says, "These are just routine questions," the poor subject is in serious trouble.

Asking good questions and then listening from a coach position (see Chapters 5 and 6) are two of your best coaching tools. But it's easy to misuse and abuse the technique when questioning becomes the third degree.

Avoid asking questions in staccato bursts, and avoid rhetorical questions, fill-in-the-blank questions, and pointed or leading questions.

- **Rhetorical questions** come with a built-in right answer. When the insurance sales representative asks if you want to be sure that your family is adequately protected when you're no longer able to bring home a paycheck, you know you're supposed to say "yes, of course." The rep is trying to get that first "yes" response to involve you in the sales pitch.

  Rhetorical questions are manipulative and don't represent honest communication. They may get you hostility instead of dialogue and cooperation. They certainly don't do much to move the conversation forward.

- **Fill-in-the-blank questions** treat the person giving the answers like a somewhat slow fifth-grader, struggling to pass a quiz.

"Who can tell us the six major trouble spots to effective coaching discussed in this chapter? Someone? Anyone?"

Pretty simple stuff, if you limit your questions to that level. It's hardly the kind of probe that would encourage a worker to enter into a serious discussion. Remember to ask a more open-ended question, like "What are some of the ways we could improve this situation?" A question like this invites brainstorming, creativity, and resourcefulness, rather than looking for a checklist of certain responses.

- **Pointed or leading questions,** like their rhetorical cousins, also carry implied "right" answers: "You wouldn't really want to do that, *would* you?" A worker wouldn't even have to know what you're talking about to know that you don't think she ought to do it. These aren't even questions really: It's an opinion (or direct order) disguised as a question.

Ask *real* questions that need real answers.

Focus on Fixing

An employee brings you a problem, and you fix it. That's your job, right? Yes and no.

Making sure the job gets done is part of your job. However, coaching employees to peak performance is a more important part of your job. This doesn't mean "fixing" them or fixing problems.

FOR EXAMPLE

PARENTING AS COACHING METAPHOR

If you have kids, then you have probably experienced the desire to "fix" things for them so that all turns out well. You've probably also learned that sometimes you have to let them try something and fail so that they can learn. A person who "learns the hard way" (with failure *and* success) is much more capable than someone who hasn't really had to try.

When a toddler learns to walk, there is a lot of wobbly balance, holding onto things, shaky steps, and falling down. Sure, you could just take his hands and walk him around with you all day. But you don't. You may set him up for success with shoes or grippy socks so he won't slip, and then take away his support so he can't hold onto anything and *must* walk. At some point, you go just beyond his reach and entice him to come to you by taking an unaided step, and then another. You cheer and applaud when he takes those steps, and encourage him to do it again and again. Yes, he'll fall down sometimes, but you can watch with pride as he gets back up and keeps going.

It may take a bit more time—and a lot more patience—to coach employees to fix problems rather than to take the problems out of their hands and do the fixing yourself. But in the long run, you'll wind up fixing the same problem time after time, all the while nurturing frustration and dependence in employees. They won't know how to do it. And they won't grow and develop if you constantly do it for them.

The Blame Game

"Hey, boss. The copy machine's jammed again."

"Who fouled it up this time?!"

Instead of fixing it yourself or, better still, coaching the employee to fix it, you spend your time and energy trying to figure out whose fault it is. You wind up with two frustrated people—you and the employee. You may or may not know who gets the blame, and you haven't done a thing to solve the problem.

Blame and shame is an endless negative spiral. Finger-pointing doesn't really solve anything, and it can quickly devolve into name calling. People start dredging up the past and focusing on the negative: "You *never* put toner in the copier, you're just lazy, and obviously you expect everyone else to do it for you!"

It may feel good, momentarily, to find a culprit and even reprimand him or her. But it does nothing to get to a solution and move forward. Keep your focus on improvement.

Failure to Follow Through

Follow-through is crucial in golf, tennis, and coaching. Coaches support their clients in a major way by providing *accountability*.

When you give an assignment or coach someone to a solution, establish clear criteria for evaluating progress and set a plan for follow-up. In less formal situations, jot yourself a reminder to check on a worker's progress. Don't wait until the deadline is past due to go looking for the producer.

Ask the employee what you can do to help her stay accountable to the tasks she committed to. She may surprise you and say, "Send me an e-mail in one week asking how it's going" or "Stop by my cubicle every day and ask for a five-second status update." Or she might want a little more independence and say something like "I will e-mail you a daily report, and just check with me if you don't receive it."

You've got the tools you need to handle problems, to prevent problems from happening, and to turn negatives into positives.

In the next chapter, we take a close look at a specific coaching session by breaking it down into component parts.

The Coach's Checklist for Chapter 11

☑ Eliminate activities that lack a purpose. They undermine your effectiveness and that of your employees.

☑ You can't avoid anxiety all the time, so recognize it and develop a personal method for handling it rather than letting it handle you.

☑ Examine your behavior and attitude. Make sure you aren't doing things that will strike fear into your employees. Fear gets in the way of communication and performance (yours and theirs).

☑ Understand why people (including you) resist change, and you can deal with the resistance to everyone's benefit.

☑ Make sure your employees really understand what you're saying. Don't use language and jargon that gets in the way of communicating clearly.

☑ Avoid one-way communication, interrogations, and the urge to personally fix all problems.

Steps to Effective Coaching

As a manager, you're responsible for making sure that work gets done promptly and properly. That's what "managing" means.

But for a supervisor who manages by coaching, getting the work done is only part of the job. The other part, sometimes the more important part, is developing employees to be able to function effectively and independently, as well as grow into new skills and abilities.

Here are the key steps to help you in this process when coaching your employees.

Step 1. Build rapport

Step 2. Identify issue or goal

Step 3. Create vision

Step 4. Brainstorm approaches

Step 5. Establish action plan

Step 6. Commitment and accountability

Step 7. Acknowledgment

Step 8. Follow-up

Note that these are tasks for you as coach, not for employees.

Does this seem like overkill—too much structure to apply to what might be a quick hallway meeting or when someone pops in your office with a question? You have to be the judge. You won't need all these steps in every situation (or they may seem to blend together and not be discrete), and you can use this process informally when the situation warrants. But be wary not to skip steps, especially the first few times you try it. This method has been tested, and it works.

To best explain the process, we use a case example.

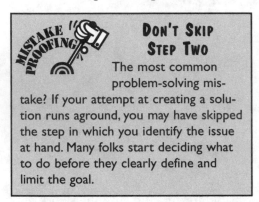

MISTAKE PROOFING

DON'T SKIP STEP TWO

The most common problem-solving mistake? If your attempt at creating a solution runs aground, you may have skipped the step in which you identify the issue at hand. Many folks start deciding what to do before they clearly define and limit the goal.

Your company has gotten too big for its parking lot, and the informal rule of "survival of the quickest" has started to create tension among the staff and some problems for individual employees.

The lot behind the building used to be more than adequate for employees. Those who got there earliest got the best spots, closest to the door, but late arrivals still had plenty of spaces to choose from.

KEY TERM **Top lieutenant** The origin of this term makes it a good choice here, despite its military use. It comes from the French words *lieu* and *tenir*, meaning "place" and "to hold." So a "lieutenant" is a place-holder, someone who takes your place when you're unable to do something. That doesn't have to be the same person for every task. In fact, as coach you should spread out special responsibilities among willing employees, depending on your needs and their abilities. (Sometimes you might choose a lieutenant because he or she needs to develop in a certain area, such as people skills or sense of organization.)

The workforce has expanded, but the parking lot hasn't. Street parking is metered, and there's a four-hour limit. There's a large garage three blocks away, but the daily cost for parking is somewhat high, as it's meant to be an hourly lot for downtown shoppers, and people don't want to walk to work in bad weather. There's a lot of grumbling. You're also getting complaints about double parking and cars blocking other cars in the lot. A new strip mall is opening two blocks away, so street parking and garage parking will only get worse.

You decide to call in your top lieutenant, Fran Quigley, and turn the problem over to her. Rather than just dumping the mess on her desk and walking away, you'll work through the eight-step process to coach her to a successful solution and develop her confidence and competence as a problem solver.

Step 1: Build Rapport

An important (and sometimes overlooked) first step in effective coaching is building *rapport*. You need to connect with the person who comes to you, and establish a space in which you can move forward together. Sometimes this means setting someone at ease, and sometimes it means matching their emotional energy. In any case, establishing rapport allows you both to play on the same field, so you'll be working together instead of at parallel or cross-purposes.

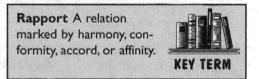

Rapport A relation marked by harmony, conformity, accord, or affinity.

KEY TERM

Professional coaches must spend time in each coaching session building rapport with a client. They do not have the luxury of working with them all day, every day, and so must create an environment of trust, openness, and creativity in the first few minutes of any coaching session.

As a manager, you know your employees very well, and this makes establishing rapport a little easier. Be sure you don't neglect this stage, assuming you can just jump right in to coaching. You may have great working relationships with your team, but if a highly agitated worker comes to you, he will need an entirely different kind of communication and response from you than he would during a quick hallway chat. A moment or two to establish the appropriate connection serves you well in moving forward. The employee will feel that you respect his or her situation, viewpoint, opinions, and even emotions. This opens the door for them to be coached effectively.

How do you establish rapport? You'll use many of the tools already discussed in this book:

- Body language that's open and invites communication; matching the body language and energy of the employee (see Chapter 4).
- Employing powerful listening strategies so that the employee feels heard and valued (see Chapter 6).
- Asking effective coaching questions with genuine curiosity (see Chapter 5).
- Focusing as much as possible on the worker and his or her worldview and capabilities (see Chapter 2).
- Possibly acknowledging and reassuring the person about his or her actions and the validity of his or her opinion and experience.

You and Fran hold a meeting in her office about the parking lot issue. As you arrive at her office, you see her wrapping up a phone call (she waves for you to come on in). You sit down, politely waiting until she finishes up. When she hangs up, she seems a bit frazzled and turns to you, asking if you're ready to start.

> **TRICKS OF THE TRADE**
>
> ## PHYSICAL SPACE
>
> Notice that we had you meeting Fran in *her* office (not yours) in this example. Sometimes, the space in which you choose to coach employees can have a big impact on rapport building. Meeting employees in their own space (when possible) physically demonstrates your willingness to be in their world with them. Meeting in your office might remind them of the hierarchy in the workplace, or make them feel as if they have to step into *your* world instead of the other way around. Alternatively, a neutral third space (a small meeting room) also works, as you can eliminate distractions from your offices, as well as offering an environment where you create the new playing field together.

Instead of jumping in immediately, you say, "Actually, I'm not in a rush. Take a moment! Get some more coffee, take a deep breath." You smile as you say it, and lean back, showing with your body how relaxed you are.

Fran grins appreciatively and gets up to refill her coffee mug. When she comes back, she is visibly calmer. She silences her cell phone and turns off her computer screen. She pulls out her notepad, ready to get to work. You begin by asking about her kids—her son had a big soccer game over the weekend, and her daughter is in the class play. She smiles, and gives you a quick update. She asks how your weekend was, and you give her a few details of your trip to the art museum to see the new exhibit.

After a little chitchat, you get down to business.

Step 2: Identify the Issue or Goal

The way you name the issue at hand largely determines how you'll try to solve it—and your chances of succeeding. In Chapter 7, we discussed at length how to create solutions (and solve problems) using a coaching framework. The techniques discussed there begin with defining the opportunity and goal, a critical step. You both need to be on the same page, or else you'll be working to different ends.

In this case, you and Fran might attribute the parking lot congestion to

- too many cars
- too few free parking spaces (lot is too small)
- poor building location
- inadequate public transportation
- uncooperative worker-commuters
- timing (everybody wants and needs to park at the same time)

These might all be aspects of the main problem—or valid ways of naming the overall issue. The point is to view the situation from as many perspectives as possible.

Don't hesitate to reiterate or restate the issue to clarify communication. You can say something as simple as, "Before we move on, I want to be absolutely sure we're on the same page! Here's what we are addressing . . . Do I have that right?"

DEFINE THE PROBLEM

TRICKS OF THE TRADE

Many people—including a lot of managers—tend to underestimate the importance of this step. After all, when everybody recognizes there's a problem, the only thing left to do is to come up with solutions. Right?

Wrong! That's a fast shortcut to an ineffective solution. This is one time when it pays to dwell on the negative. In fact, you might even want to take an hour or so to walk around, asking for input from employees who drive to work. It's a quick way to get a variety of perspectives, so that you can better understand the problem. You might be surprised at what you learn.

When you've clarified the problem, you'll need to check and make sure it's something within your control to do something about. In the parking lot dilemma, you and Fran examine the list of contributing factors and quickly realize what you can and can't change. You *can't change* the location of the building, availability of public transit, or availability of free parking on the street or in the garage (at least not in the short run). You *can* influence the number of cars needing to use the lot, the timing of business hours, and possibly the cooperation of your employees. Focus on what is changeable so that you have effective brainstorming later.

You come up with the following description of the desired solution: *Ameliorate congestion in on-site company parking lot.*

Step 3: Create Vision

Before getting into the nitty-gritty of brainstorming action items, it pays to take a moment to imagine what you are trying to do when you work at solving the problem. This is a key aspect of coaching: creating the positive vision.

This doesn't have to be a difficult or time-consuming step. After defining the issue at hand, you can then explore what the changes might be, and how it impacts individuals, your department, the whole company, and beyond.

You ask Fran, "So, if we come up with a good solution to the parking issue, what happens then? What do you think will change around here?"

SMART

MANAGING

WORST-CASE SCENARIO

Many people have difficulty imagining positive possibilities because they tend to think in terms of disaster and catastrophe. You'll notice this when they dwell on the negative a lot, complain incessantly, or constantly come up with objections on why things *won't* work.

When this occurs in coaching, it's okay to let the person go ahead and imagine the worst-case scenario. But then challenge them to imagine the *best*-case scenario. You can say, "All right, that's the *worst* that could happen. What if everything went *right?*" or "All right, that's what you *don't* want to happen. What *do* you want to happen?" They may need encouragement and guidelines in framing things in the positive. Point out that the reality of what happens falls somewhere in between the best- and worst-case scenarios.

Fran thinks and says, "Well, I think the grumbling will quiet down! Maybe folks would be happier when they arrive at work, if they haven't had to scramble for a spot. So many people come in grumpy right now! I'd like to have a more positive environment to start the day, for all of us."

Step 4: Brainstorm Approaches

You've built rapport, defined the issue at hand, and gotten a vision of what you want to accomplish. Now you start brainstorming action steps to creating the solution you want (see Chapter 7 for some guidelines on effective brainstorming). At this phase, you're throwing out ideas for moving forward and not worrying about what you'll choose to do just yet.

Brainstorming opens up the creativity of you and your employee, and sometimes you get a synergistic effect by the two of you working together. You'll tap into knowledge, expertise, viewpoint, awareness, and information flowing from both of you.

Remember the two basic principles for effective brainstorming:

■ Uncouple the idea from the person offering the idea. You're the boss, but in a brainstorming session, you and the employee are equals.

■ Don't judge any idea until you've listed all the options you can come up with.

You and Fran may not be able to do anything substantial about some of the contributing factors to the parking problem (public transportation, building location), at least not right away. (However, you do consider some options for approaching these issues later.) You want a solution to the parking mess *now*.

You might be able to influence the "rush hour" fight for parking spaces. Staggering work hours might help the problem. In fact, management has discussed that possibility, along with flex time, job sharing, and working from home (telecommuting) as ways to improve productivity and employee morale (as well as parking). But you've been told that any major change initiative is at least a year away (a pilot program is in place testing telecommuting in one department, but it has only just started).

After working together for a few minutes, you and Fran come up with the following description of the overall thrust of the action plan:

Reduce or eliminate parking congestion by developing alternatives to single-passenger car commuting among company employees.

After the two of you spend a little time shooting out more specific ideas, you come up with several potential approaches, with a few variations on each.

- Stronger enforcement to eliminate double parking and the use of the lot by nonemployees—signage, threats, fines, towing
- Expand the parking lot—onto adjacent land, or build private parking garage
- Carpools—voluntary? mandatory?
- Encouragement of alternative transportation—bike club, covered bike rack, discount bus passes
- Assigned parking spaces—by seniority? distance driven from work? job classification?

Now you can discuss, sort, and judge those approaches. You rule out stronger enforcement almost immediately. Not only would it have little effect on the underlying problem of too many cars for too few spaces, but it would create new problems, in terms of employee resentment and frustration (and possibly pushing away customers and clients as well). Why punish employees for trying to cope with a situation that's beyond their control?

Expanding the parking lot also won't work—there's no available land to expand onto, and creating a multistory garage on the existing lot is prohibitively expensive.

Mandatory carpools carry potential for backlash and raise the problem of enforcement. What's the "or else" for a worker who refuses to share a car? Besides, what happens to employees who regularly stay late to finish a project? If they're required to carpool, you lose their flexibility and maybe undermine their commitment to doing a better job.

Trying to encourage voluntary carpooling starts to sound like a viable option, especially because almost everybody comes and goes at the same times.

Although both you and Fran like the idea of encouraging voluntary carpooling, you continue to discuss other options.

What about assigned parking spaces? That idea may be feasible and simple to implement, but it has some subtle serious side effects. In fact, when Fran offered it during brainstorming, you had to fight the urge to reject it. "Just write it down," you reminded yourself. "Don't judge. Not yet."

In light of the company's commitment to bottom-up management and the elimination of caste systems in the workplace, assigned spaces would be a step backward in the move toward greater equality.

A "bike to work" program also sounds promising, but before investing time and money in the possibility of encouraging employees to commute by bike—at least in the warmer months—you decide to create a worker survey, asking how many employees own bikes, live within feasible biking distance, and would consider biking to work. You realize that this kind of program needs more time to be developed with full company support, because you'll need to allow for physical capabilities and safety issues (some of the streets leading to your site are quite busy, a situation that will get worse with the new shopping area). Also, some employees would probably look less professional after biking several miles on a warm summer morning. This idea is put on the back burner for future development.

You also decide to check with the city transportation department regarding the possibility of getting discount bus ticket books for employees and checking with upper management on the possibility of the company subsidizing all or part of the cost of the passes. You then realize that you can approach the owners of the paid parking garage and find out about arranging a monthly parking pass for employees, possibly subsidized by the company, but in any case with a substantial discount.

"Whatever system we work out," Fran said, laughing, "we'll have to deal with those idiotic delivery vans."

Good point. Despite your company's best attempts at diplomacy with the drivers, delivery vans are constantly angled across two spaces, blocking doors and walkways, or keeping employees from going out for lunch.

"Let's assign them spaces someplace in the next county," you suggest, with a grin.

Then the light bulb goes on above Fran's head: "How about a loading zone, right out in front of the building?"

"We could create a 15-minute area . . ."

TRICKS OF THE TRADE

It's OK to Be Dumb

The worst ideas—the dumbest, most irresponsible, unworkable ones, the ones said in jest, the stand-up comic kind of ideas—often trigger really creative thoughts, the ones that work. That's why you don't want to reject anything during brainstorming. Just keep them coming, keep building on them, keep playing with them, and see what develops.

"We'd get the vans out of the lot. That would help some."

After just a few minutes of focused brainstorming, followed by a little critical analysis, you and Fran have come up with a number of possible approaches to the perplexing parking problem. You're feeling pretty good and ready to move forward.

Step 5: Establish Action Plan

Create a simple to-do list for the chosen course of action. Next to each task, note who will take responsibility for making sure it gets done. Be very clear about who does what.

For the parking problem, the list might look like this.

1. Mark employee residences on an area map and create sign-up lists for voluntary carpooling. (Fran's assistant, Gerald)
2. Hang the map in the break room with the sign-up lists. (Gerald)
3. Put an article on the company intranet and online newsletter talking up the benefits of carpooling. (Fran)
4. Check with upper management about the possibility of establishing a 15-minute delivery zone in front of the building. (You)
5. Create and send out a survey to determine to what extent employees are able and willing to consider biking to work. (Fran)
6. Check with the city transportation department about getting discount bus tickets. (You)
7. Check with parking garage owners about monthly parking passes. (You)
8. Get the subject of bus subsidies on the agenda for the next upper management meeting. (You)

Deadlines

Don't duck the all-important question of "*when*?" Without a specific deadline, a task may never become a priority, so it may not get done—or

---

CONTRACT DEADLINES

SMART

A big advantage to setting deadlines is that it saves time and worry. If you only make a mental note to take care of something, you're likely to think about it from time to time and worry about getting around to it. That can distract you from your other responsibilities and the **MANAGING** "mental note" will get pushed to the back burner because there's no time limit. Plus, the more you worry about a task, the more likely you are to put it off and then finally to do it quickly, just to get it off your mind.

Think of setting deadlines as signing a contract with your project partners.

---

it may be done in haste, when somebody thinks to ask about it. Set a deadline for each item on the to-do list. Better still, write down exactly when you intend to do the task.

Don't just stop at picking a deadline—*schedule* when you will take action, writing down when you will do each step! If it's on your calendar to do in steps (i.e., "research bus pass rates, find appropriate contact information for the city, schedule meeting, hold meeting"), you're more likely to get to work, rather than just seeing the deadline of when it has to be done and trying to jam it all in at the last minute.

Establish Criteria for Evaluation

An important step in developing an action plan is to establish criteria for evaluation. Make sure you know exactly what outcomes you want and how you'll know when you get them.

Your major focus in the case example is carpooling. You need to answer some questions to create your evaluation guidelines. How many people need to start sharing rides for the program to be a success? How will you know they're actually doing it? Don't get off the track here by thinking that "20 percent is a good participation rate for anything in this company" or "we'd be doing well to get 100 employees involved." Think in terms of your *goal*. Will 20 percent be enough, and how would you know you've reached this level? More to the point, how many cars will those 100 employees be sharing—50, 30, 25? How much will that improve the parking situation? How much will you need to count on bikes and buses?

In this case, you and Fran decide on specific evaluation criteria for determining whether the parking problem solutions are successful:

> **HELP, DON'T INTRUDE**
>
> **CAUTION** The operative word with your employees is *facilitate*, which means "to make it easier." Avoid the temptation to help too much. Some managers tend to intrude and assume that the assigned employee wants help. That's not a safe assumption—and often a dangerous one. There are times when it might seem best to take over a task and "fix" it. That's paternalistic managing and about as far away from coaching as you can get.
>
> Let employees know that you're there if they need you. But leave that decision to them.

- 20 percent of workforce committing to voluntary carpooling (counted by checking the sign-up sheets for number of names, and conducting surveys to find out who is carpooling and the results)
- creation of the loading zone (easily evaluated—it's either done or not done)
- survey response of at least 20 employees interested in biking to work
- survey response of at least 20 employees interested in the discounted bus passes (assessed through a survey, delivered next month)

Step 6: Commitment and Accountability

"Let's make it happen!" Part of coaching involves getting commitment to the action plan. In the workplace, this is often implied because tasks have been assigned, so they "must" be done. Even so, taking a moment to get a clear statement of commitment can really serve everyone involved. You don't have to get corny and pretend to be a cheerleader, saying "Let's go, team!" A simple "Ready to get to work?" will serve fine.

Don't forget your *own* commitment. What can you as manager do to help employees succeed? Restate your commitments from the action plan, if need be.

You've already gotten involved by taking on the tasks most appropriate for you. Consider, too, anything Fran might need to help her get her tasks done. Maybe you could give her a few quotes for her article on carpooling to show that management is supportive and involved in solving the parking problem. How about Gerald? Would he like you to informally talk with the employees and encourage them to sign up to carpool? To show your commitment here, you can say, "All right, I'll get to work on those tidbits for your article, and I'll connect with Gerald to give him the information he needs. I'll work on getting in touch with the transit authority and parking garage folks in two weeks. I'm excited about this plan!"

Sometimes the best way to facilitate action is to hold your team members *accountable* for their commitments. Just being the person they report to is sometimes enough to motivate people to get to work and stay on track. Other times, you might need to dangle a reward of some sort to provide some motivation.

In this case, you decide that if the carpooling program is successful, you'll reward Fran and Gerald with gift cards to the local coffee shop (where they both love to get a morning cup of java). If the program succeeds beyond the goal of 20 percent—say, if you get to 30 percent or more—involvement in carpooling, you'll *double* the amounts of the gift cards. When you tell Fran this, you see a gleam in her eye.

Step 7: Acknowledgment

Acknowledgment after a coaching session often gets overlooked in the rush to get out the door and get down to business. Hopefully, you've said "nice work!" or "good idea!" along the way. You should consider taking another moment to recognize the work of the employee who was coached. Don't just focus on their accomplishments—point out what impressed you overall. How did they respond to being coached as opposed to being told what to do? Were they creative, resourceful, knowledgeable, engaged, and invested? If you comment on these things, the employee will *know* you listened and valued his or her input. You'll demonstrate the value you put on these big-picture characteristics. And you'll be more likely to see those positive aspects in the workplace.

As you finish up, you turn to Fran and thank her for her time. You add, "I noticed a lot of creative responses from you, and I appreciate that! I think we brainstorm well together. You put forth some ideas I certainly wouldn't have thought of, and I can't wait to see how they get put to use!" She smiles a little bashfully, but seems happy that you've noticed her contribution.

Step 8: Follow-Up

As we've discussed in this book, follow-up is a critical part of any action plan, and it's no different with coaching. If you haven't already crafted a plan for follow-up, make sure you do so before the end of the meeting. Follow-up plays a big role in accountability for a lot of people. Plus, you can use follow-up steps to track progress, change, and success.

The idea isn't to create an endless chain of meetings. (We all know how that tends to bog down any project!) But you do need to ensure accountability to keep well-intentioned plans from getting lost in the day-to-day shuffle and other crises of the moment. It's a way of collaboratively enforcing the deadlines. Also, employees who might be hesitant to come talk with you about questions or concerns are more likely to bring them up when they report on their progress.

You set a time to get back together with Fran for a progress report. You figure that after two weeks, you'll have most of the steps done and will be ready to evaluate how those steps went, what was learned along the way, and launch the carpooling (and evaluation) program.

The Coach's Checklist for Chapter 12

- ☑ If you want to use coaching effectively, you'll need a consistent process for working with your employees.
- ☑ Step 1 is building rapport, to set the tone for coaching.
- ☑ Step 2 is making things happen: Identify the issue or goal and describe the desired outcome. Don't forget to define it accurately.
- ☑ Step 3 involves creating a positive vision of what you want to accomplish.
- ☑ Step 4: Brainstorm possible approaches. Don't forget to encourage people to be open and maybe even a little outrageous. It triggers creativity.
- ☑ Step 5: Establish an action plan. Assign responsibilities, deadlines, and criteria for evaluation.
- ☑ Step 6: Get commitment and accountability. Facilitate action. Figure out what your employees need to successfully complete their tasks. Hold them accountable.

☑ Step 7: Acknowledge the good work of your employees, especially their work during the coaching session.

☑ Step 8: Follow-up. Make sure what's supposed to happen by your deadlines does happen.

Once More,
with Feedback

"**H**ow am I doing?"

It's one of the most natural questions in the world. We all wonder how others judge us, whether they like or approve of us in a social setting and whether our performance measures up in the workplace. Just because we're too cool (or too nervous) to ask doesn't mean we don't want and need to know.

What if someone significant in your life, someone with the power to determine your future, gave you feedback on your performance only once each year, and then only in a general way. Ridiculous, right? Yet many people work day in and day out without any meaningful feedback other than an annual performance review, which is too often a perfunctory exercise in paper shuffling.

Consider the people who work with you. Do you give them regular, meaningful feedback on their work? If not, you're missing one of the best coaching opportunities—and a great chance to help improve performance and create a positive, dynamic environment for growth.

Elements of Effective Feedback

The ability to offer effective feedback is essential to good managing. It also opens the door for powerful coaching opportunities, and gives your employees a chance to grow, beyond just "fixing" issues or accomplishing a particular goal. Let's look at some of the elements of effective feedback.

Positive, Negative, and Neutral Comments

"I only hear from him when I screw up."

"I close 99 sales in a row, and I don't hear a murmur from the front office. But the minute one slips away, all hell breaks loose."

"Sometimes I wonder if I ever do anything right around here!"

Do these comments sound familiar? (If not, then you're working in the only ideal company in the country.) Far too often, we only get feedback when something has gone wrong.

For too many workers, "feedback" means "criticism." Constant criticism is seldom effective in coaching workers to peak performance and, in fact, may suppress performance as workers labor to hide their mistakes and avoid contact with supervisors. It also wears on their self-esteem and can disengage them. They don't feel valued or valuable if they only hear from you when there is a problem.

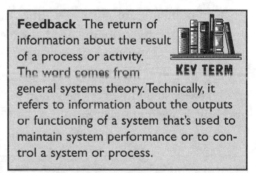

Feedback The return of information about the result of a process or activity. The word comes from general systems theory. Technically, it refers to information about the outputs or functioning of a system that's used to maintain system performance or to control a system or process.

KEY TERM

That sounds very mechanical. Certainly no manager, especially one who coaches, wants to treat employees as if they were merely components in a system. After all, they're human beings, not machines. But with machines at least you get feedback continually, both negative and positive.

Negative feedback is only one aspect of the total range of responses to a worker's efforts, and it's necessary and sometimes unavoidable. Feedback should include praise for work well done and for honest effort that fails to yield results through no fault of the worker. Often, a worker just needs to hear about the unseen results of her efforts, a simple reporting of outcomes with neither criticism nor praise attached.

THE SANDWICH TECHNIQUE

TOOLS

If you have to deliver negative feedback, try using a "sandwich" technique. Begin with something positive, pointing out what the worker did well. Then, deliver the bad news. Wrap up with another positive statement. You might say, "Dan, you did a great job with the Greene account, and the executives were impressed! I have to tell you that your work on the Williams proposal was not your best—the terms were unclear and the client went with another agency. However, the feedback from the Romer project is excellent, and the clients specifically tell us how great your communication has been." This works well with short, quick notes of feedback. If you have to go into detail on why the Williams proposal was not Dan's best work, you should have a sit-down, face-to-face session.

Timeliness

"Remember that presentation you made last June? You know, the pitch to the buyers from McConnell? I thought it was very effective. Right on target. Nice going."

Compliments are great any time. But the further the compliment becomes separated from the deed, the less emotional impact it will have. The recipient of the compliment might even doubt your motives, thinking you are softening him or her up before delivering a blow of bad news.

Likewise, the longer a suggestion for improvement follows performance, the less effect it will have.

"Gee, if I'd known how the boss felt about my presentation, I would

GIVE MY BEST TO SPARKY

You'll likely make some big mistakes if you only think big. Smart managers think in terms of the big picture, of the company as a system, of teamwork. But they remember to connect with individuals. Managers create that critical link between the big picture and the team on the ground.

If possible, walk around the workplace regularly, providing feedback—especially positive feedback—to each employee.

If that's not feasible, how about e-mail? It's easy enough to write a quick message and send it off in seconds. Customize a note for each individual. You can add a simple comment like "Give your dog a scratch behind the ears for me!" or "By the way, I hope Meg is enjoying soccer." It's a great chance to show how well you know the employees and establish rapport.

have been more confident when I did my pitch for the Archer account—and maybe we would have won that account."

Whether it's negative or positive or (most likely) both, link your feedback as closely as possible to the behavior you're commenting on.

Individual Recognition

Employees take pride in playing on an effective team and share in the reflected glory of a team victory. But that doesn't mean they don't appreciate recognition for their individual efforts and achievements in the team's success. Quite the contrary!

A form memo addressed to "members of the task force committee" doesn't mean nearly as much as a personal note to each person on the committee, even if each member of the group gets one—as long as the notes don't say exactly the same thing.

Likewise, general comments about "poor overall performance" to a group of workers will have little effect on any one person. It's human nature to ascribe low team achievement to the other guy or to "bad chemistry." Too often, the people who need the change won't see that such a message is directed at them.

KNOW WHAT YOU'RE PRAISING

SMART MANAGING

Marilyn was a wonderful person, and she wanted to be a wonderful vice president. She took a few moments from time to time to walk around and chat with the employees.

She emphasized the positive, saying such things as "Good job!" and "Hey, I like the way we're all working together!" The workers appreciated her comments, but they all knew that she was more or less clueless about how any individual was actually performing—and sometimes even about what a certain worker was assigned to do.

The moral of the story: Praise is good, but specific praise means much more and is far more effective.

Specific Examples

The best way to individualize feedback is to refer to specific, unique behaviors.

Which comment would seem more credible to you if you read it in a letter of recommendation for a potential hire—a series of general refer-

Put It in Writing

When you have a specific example of excellent performance for a particular worker, put it in writing. Don't stop with e-mail or a memo, which is a great start. Make sure that the employee's personnel file includes a written comment about the success, or write a recommendation for the person on LinkedIn, if you both use it. This is one of the ways you can help your employees grow into new positions. Many times, workers are too shy to ask for such a favor, so you should be proactive in making it happen.

ences to the worker being "dependable" and a "self-starter," or specific examples of projects he or she carried out effectively and independently?

Specific examples carry more weight. They put generic phrases into real-life terms. They *demonstrate* (not just tell) what a person is capable of.

The same goes for any feedback you give on job performance. Refer to specific actions and outcomes. Otherwise, even praise sounds empty and vague.

Sincerity

Say what you mean, mean what you say, and say it like you mean it.

Sincerity is equal parts speaking truth and speaking it honestly. Your feedback must be genuine, and you must deliver it in a way that is natural and authentic for you.

Empty praise is no more effective than chronic carping. Employees learn to screen out and disregard both.

Keep Track of Good Work

If you manage a large number of employees or if you have memory problems, take notes.

You might use index cards or business cards (or any sort of digital reminder system). Put the name of an employee on each card and alphabetize the cards. Whenever you get input about an employee, jot it down on his or her card. If you hear a comment like "Marge stayed late Friday to finish that paperwork" or "Gee, Terry almost fell asleep at the switch this morning," or if you read in the company newsletter that Bert has volunteered to head up the United Way drive, make a note.

Then, take the next opportunity to compliment Marge and Bert or express your concern to Terry. Glance at the note to refresh your memory, and you're ready to go.

Don't try to adopt a "management style" when delivering feedback. The best style for you is your own natural manner of speaking and acting, without forced mannerisms or studied inflections. Be yourself, and the feedback will flow authentically and comfortably for you.

What's the best way to be natural? Practice! That may seem contradictory, but it makes sense. Here's a suggestion. When you're at home, make a point of stopping in front of the mirror and complimenting yourself. It may seem silly at first. But study your reflection. How do you look? How do you sound? Sincere? Natural? Try complimenting your friends, family, and other people you know. Notice their reaction.

Work at being yourself. Just a minute or two from time to time can make a big difference in your style—and make your feedback to employees more effective.

Before You Deliver Feedback

Before letting someone know how he or she is doing, take a few moments to gather your thoughts and decide on the best way to deliver your message. The guidelines discussed in this section will help you make that decision.

Think before you speak. What? How? Why?

Effective feedback takes preparation. Think about what you want to say, how you want to say it, and what effect you intend for it to have. It's best not to just blurt out feedback.

But feedback must also be timely, right? We're not talking about a month-long deliberation here. Preparation time for effective feedback is often minutes or even seconds, but it's important that you take those seconds to consider what, how, and why.

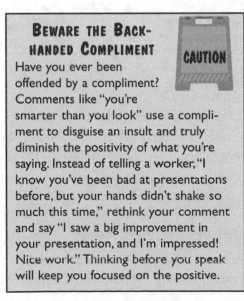

BEWARE THE BACK-HANDED COMPLIMENT

CAUTION

Have you ever been offended by a compliment? Comments like "you're smarter than you look" use a compliment to disguise an insult and truly diminish the positivity of what you're saying. Instead of telling a worker, "I know you've been bad at presentations before, but your hands didn't shake so much this time," rethink your comment and say "I saw a big improvement in your presentation, and I'm impressed! Nice work." Thinking before you speak will keep you focused on the positive.

Say it face-to-face. No doubt you have to fill out performance reports, write memos, and create many types of written evaluations of your employees. Creating a paper trail (or e-trail) is necessary in the workplace. But reports, memos, and written evaluations rarely match the effectiveness of the spoken word, delivered in person. Don't hide behind paper, the phone, or e-mail. If possible, say it with your *presence* as well as your words. Use the written word to back up what you're saying.

Go one-on-one. Two is feedback. Three is a performance.

The presence of witnesses alters your message in ways you can't always control. Criticism delivered in public isn't feedback—it's punishment. It's also humiliating, and folks don't tend to learn anything helpful while being blamed and shamed.

SMART

MANAGING

PRAISE IN PUBLIC, CRITICIZE IN PRIVATE

That bit of folk wisdom has guided wise supervisors for ages, and it's still a worthy guide in many situations. You'll have to judge when public praise will serve your overall goal of coaching for peak performance. Private criticism reduces shame and offers an opportunity for more collaborative work to move forward and correct the issue.

Praising workers in front of their peers can be a real ego booster, of course, but for some it can be almost as embarrassing as criticism, as it focuses attention on them, and they may not be comfortable with that. It may also cause resentment among other workers. Public praise of one may seem like implied criticism of the others. (For some, it may dredge up old fears of being scorned by other kids as a teacher's pet.)

Here's another reason not to go public with individual feedback: You're only human. Whether you're delivering good news or bad, you'll naturally tend to aim that delivery at least in part at the whole audience. Playing to the crowd may be human nature, but it's not an effective feedback technique.

Delivering Bad News

How do you feel about delivering bad news? If you're like most managers, you may feel that it's the part of your job that takes the most out of you. It's not easy to tell someone they screwed up. In fact, we often dread it, and put it off or avoid it altogether.

You can't avoid it, of course. If you try to dodge the responsibility, you're likely to make matters worse—and develop a reputation that will make you less effective. But you can certainly learn how to handle a bad-news situation.

Above all, you need to avoid an adversarial tone. Setting up a boss–employee confrontation only creates resistance and resentment, not better work. Let's look at some ways to deliver bad news effectively.

1. Select an appropriate environment. The setting may be as important as the message. Where you choose to deliver the message becomes part of the communication.

Consider using the employee's own space—office, cubicle, or work station—as long as it's *private*. Playing the feedback game on the worker's home court strips you of the trappings of power, which means that the roar of your authority won't drown out your words. Employees tend to feel more relaxed in their own area and thus are a little less likely to become easily inflamed.

THE ROUND TABLE

SMART

MANAGING

"First among peers." That was the title of the person who may have been the first manager-coach, King Arthur.

Sure, he was the king, the CEO of his country. But when he met with his knights, his lieutenants, he made sure to emphasize equality. He didn't sit on his throne. He didn't stand over them or make them drop to their knees. And he certainly did not hide behind a tree.

He gathered his employees around a table that had no head, no place of honor, no physical sign that he was their superior. That team was known as the Knights of the Round Table and King Arthur gained a reputation for leading his teammates as "first among peers."

This approach, fit for a king, is certainly fit for any manager.

If you decide to call the employee into your office, invite him or her to sit down and then resist the temptation to remain standing (elevating yourself while diminishing the employee), sit on your "throne" (a better, higher chair), or retreat behind your desk or other barrier.

You might also select a neutral site. If so, be sure to choose a pleasant place, not a public thoroughfare where you're likely to be interrupted or a

---

> **DON'T STALL**
>
> "Drawing on shared purpose" doesn't mean a long oration on the history of the organization or a thorough review of the mission statement. It probably doesn't even mean talking at length about how all members of the staff are working together toward a common goal.
>
> A little small talk may, of course, help relax both of you and build some rapport. But the longer you delay coming to the point, the more tension you create. Employees know you didn't call them in to talk about the weather.

messy storage area. A private meeting room can help remove any distractions from computers and phones, and offer a focused, neutral space for collaborative communication.

2. Talk from common goals. Draw on your shared purpose, the goals that unite you in the work you do. Ultimately, you both want the same thing (peak performance). Explain how you intend your comments to serve that purpose.

>
>
> **SMART**
>
> **BE REASONABLE!**
>
> **MANAGING**
>
> You're the boss! Why do you need to give reasons for your decisions, especially to an employee who has been performing poorly or behaving badly?
>
> Consider it an investment in your employees and yourself.
>
> Think about it. If you decide to terminate an employee, everybody will know how you handled the situation. Whether or not they believe you made the right decision to punish or terminate that person, they will wonder whether you'll stop being a reasonable, fair manager if any of them happens to cross some line. In other words, they're likely to identify with that employee, and that reaction could hurt your work culture.
>
> Handling this situation in a fair and reasonable way allows you the opportunity to really test your commitment to being an effective coach and a smart manager.

3. Offer reasons. It isn't so just because you *say* it's so.

This exchange isn't an inquisition. You aren't a prosecuting attorney, marshalling evidence to get a conviction, nor are you a logician, "proving" a point. Don't hound an employee, asking why something went wrong (if you need to know, ask *how* it happened, not why).

> ## DON'T NAME NAMES
>
> When offering your reasons for delivering bad news, be sure you don't point fingers in other directions. You can explain the reasons behind your conclusions, but at no point should you compare one worker to another or mention that a specific person complained. If you say, "Why can't you be more like Bill?" or "Sarah said you made an inappropriate call to the client." You have only sowed discord in your team (the employee now thinks "Bill's a goody-goody and Sarah's a tattletale!"), while abdicating your own responsibility (you're implying that you don't think these things, you are just passing along the news). You can rephrase such statements as "I would like to see you improve your time management skills" or "I understand that you may have made a call to a client that was not within our guidelines, and we need to talk about it."

But you are the boss, and as boss, you bear the burden of explaining why you've reached the conclusion that performance is lacking or behavior is inappropriate. Explain the "why" as you deliver the "what."

4. Speak to *their* needs. You've got your reasons for delivering this feedback. What are their reasons for listening?

Applying a coach approach here is valuable. Spend a moment creating a positive vision of what things will be like when they improve—for the employee, you, the department, the company. How will your comments help them do their jobs better? How will that improved performance help them grow and possibly advance?

If you don't have ready answers to these questions, think about them first. You'll provide more useful information, and you'll stand a better chance of getting the results you want.

Ask yourself, "What's in this for *them*?" to frame your comments.

5. Talk about *actions*, not motives. You're a manager/coach, not a therapist or a parole officer. You're coaching performance, not personality. Confine your message to what they do, not who they are.

Remember that you don't really know who they are. As a supervisor, you must gather enough information to accurately judge how they perform. But any conclusions about the motives behind that performance are most likely just speculation.

Inappropriate comment: "You're lazy."

SMART MANAGING

TAP INTO THE POSITIVE
When delivering negative feedback, focus on actions instead of motives or identity, as mentioned. When coaching someone to maximum performance, *then* you want to connect with who they are! Change becomes sustainable when the person connects it to a bigger reason, and actions begin to flow from who the person is, rather than simply what they do.

Appropriate comment: "You've missed your quota the last two weeks."

Let the worker tell you why or how—if it's useful to the discussion.

6. Assume your fair share of responsibility. The employees didn't follow your instructions. They heard them. They agreed with them (or at least they said they did). But they still didn't carry them out, or didn't do so satisfactorily.

Be open to the possibility that you didn't explain clearly what you wanted them to do or might have missed another step in your responsibilities. It takes two to communicate—not just a willing receiver but also an effective sender. Your message is effective only if it gets the desired result. If you promised them tools or support and didn't deliver, you're just as much at fault.

"I didn't get the message across" may be a better way to begin the discussion than "You didn't get the message."

This isn't a matter of being nice. It's a matter of being effective and not making a bad situation worse.

7. Provide choices, options, and opportunities. If you've been clear, compelling, and compassionate in explaining how the worker has missed the mark, it's time to explore what he or she can and should do to perform better. Remember: Your goal here isn't to punish but to improve performance. This is when you start coaching.

First, ask the employee about his or her opinion on what should be done (use the coaching framework discussed throughout this book). If you have a specific plan in mind, lay it out and give the worker the chance to buy into the plan or modify it. Ask for suggestions. End the session only when both of you know exactly what should happen next.

Feedback on Your Feedback

We began this chapter with one of the most natural questions in the world—"How am I doing?"

Employees need to know the answer to that question, and you need to know whether you're doing your job well, too.

The best way to judge how effectively you're communicating with employees is to observe their subsequent performance. But you can benefit

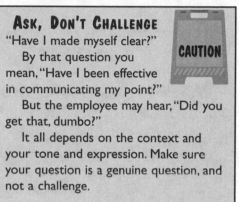

ASK, DON'T CHALLENGE

"Have I made myself clear?"

By that question you mean, "Have I been effective in communicating my point?"

But the employee may hear, "Did you get that, dumbo?"

It all depends on the context and your tone and expression. Make sure your question is a genuine question, and not a challenge.

from more immediate feedback on your feedback. Here are some ways to get it.

- **Keep conversations open-ended.** Don't lecture. Encourage dialogue. Use receptive body language—arms loose at your sides rather than crossed over your chest, for example. Pause frequently so that employees can reply without having to interrupt. (Some people are reluctant to interrupt others, especially if it's the boss.)
- **Ask for feedback.** Asking an employee for an opinion or observation does not in any way diminish your authority. If anything, it enhances

it. If you want to know, ask. However, if you don't want to hear the answer, don't ask the question.

"Tell me what you really think" can mean what it says. It can also mean "Tell me that you agree with me."

Don't ask for feedback because you think it's the right thing to do or you think you

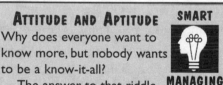

ATTITUDE AND APTITUDE SMART

Why does everyone want to know more, but nobody wants to be a know-it-all?

The answer to that riddle comes down to the letter p. MANAGING

The difference between knowing more and being a know-it-all is the difference between *aptitude* and *attitude*. The more you know, the greater your aptitude. But acting like you know it all is an attitude—and it will keep you from learning.

should. Don't ask because you read in a management book that you're supposed to. You may only trick the employee into beginning a conversation you don't want to have. If you then show no interest in the reply, the employee may feel betrayed. If you work hard at building trust, don't undermine your efforts by betraying that trust, even unintentionally.

Be open about your knowledge gaps. You *don't* know everything. Don't pretend you do.

Information should flow in both directions. You'll enhance your authority and assure your employees that you want to be fair by asking for input when you need it.

Accept employees' comments without judgment. The words "You're welcome to your opinion" shouldn't be followed by "but ..." They also shouldn't be dripping with scorn or sarcasm.

First, all employees are entitled to their opinions, whether or not you agree with them or like them. Second, if you show you're not really open to their comments, you're going to get fewer of them. Employees won't risk a cold reception (although some may relish the chance to put a thorn in your side).

Don't get defensive, and don't get drawn into an argument. Nobody ever wins that kind of battle, and an argument *will* undermine your authority. Accept contrary opinions. Agree to disagree as to causes or blame.

You're not infallible. You're not all-knowing. But you are the boss. That title is certainly no guarantee of perfection, but it does mean that you're responsible for your team of employees. In fact, that's what Harry S. Truman meant when he said, "The buck stops here." A good manager doesn't claim to be omniscient. A good manager just recognizes where the buck stops.

Feedback is essential to effective managing. Good feedback is personal and sincere and, like all coaching behaviors, intended to foster peak performance. Feedback combined with coaching can create an environment for a lot of positive change.

The Coach's Checklist for Chapter 13

☑ Feedback is important. If you want your employees to know how they're doing, you have to tell them.

☑ Don't just tell employees when they've made a mistake. Make sure you deliver positive feedback as well. That's how your employees will know what you like. Make your feedback timely.

☑ Praise the team, but don't forget that individuals like praise for their achievements as well.

☑ Make sure your feedback is specific. General or vague feedback doesn't mean much.

☑ Be sincere. Say what you mean, mean what you say, and say it like you mean it.

☑ Before you deliver feedback, think before you speak, say it face to face, and go one-on-one.

☑ Know how to deliver bad news. Don't make it a confrontation.

Coaching and Rewards

R eward the performance you want. Positive reinforcement is far more effective than punishment when something goes wrong. To use a carrot-and-stick analogy, where you mix positive and negative reinforcement, dangle a carrot (positive reward) at least 85 percent of the time. Wield the stick (punishment) the other 15 percent.

It sounds so simple, and yet many managers fail to follow this basic principle of rewarding the preferred behavior. Most often, they seem to ignore competence and focus attention only on performance or behaviors they don't like.

When that happens, it may discourage peak performance. Employees decide there's not much incentive to do better than meet the standards. And you're going to be spending a lot of time correcting, criticizing, and even punishing. This "blame and shame" spiral is ultimately unproductive, as it keeps people in finger-pointing mode. If you're always worried about doing something wrong, you probably won't make the extra effort to be truly excellent. You're more likely to focus on not screwing up. This mindset in a corporate environment works to disengage employees and create an "every man for himself" kind of atmosphere.

So, it's important to know about using rewards in your role as manager/coach. A professional coach does not offer rewards per se to clients, but in your role as manager, you can incorporate rewards with your coach approach to make them meaningful.

Let's take a look at the three basic kinds of rewards you can use to encourage peak performance: tangible, symbolic, and intangible.

POSITIVE FOCUS

TRICKS OF THE TRADE

Throughout this book, we've talked about focusing on the *positive*, on what you *want*. If your employees are always worried about making mistakes, they are focusing on the negative. Challenge them (and yourself) to focus on what they do *right* and do well, and build from that. Sure, there will be mistakes sometimes, and you can address those, also in a positive framework. It takes time to establish this kind of groupthink in a corporate culture, but be persistent.

Tangible Rewards

"Show me the money!" This catchphrase from *Jerry Maguire* went from cliché to parody at warp speed. This was because it so perfectly expressed an almost universally held sentiment: If you want my best effort and my loyalty, pay me big bucks.

Money is certainly the most obvious of tangible rewards for peak performance in the workplace. What some managers don't realize is that an increase in compensation or a bonus serves as a reward for meritorious service only if they're clearly linked to the performance and are unique. And for a growing number of employees (especially Millennials or Generation Y), money is no longer a prime motivator.

If everyone in the job classification gets an identical (or nearly identical) annual raise or bonus—regardless of performance—it simply becomes a step increase, a cost-of-living increase, a token effort at reward, or a way to keep employees if the market is paying better elsewhere. You've rewarded longevity, not specific performance. (This is a lot like everyone getting an honorable mention just for competing in a contest!) You're encouraging employees to stick around and survive, but not to thrive.

Advancement in rank (promotion) stands with a raise in pay or bonus as a powerful tangible reward. In fact, they're often linked. During wartime,

> **Promotion** The original meaning was "movement forward," as when soldiers were asked to move ahead of their comrades and assume leadership responsibilities. Unfortunately, this
> **KEY TERM** word is currently used only in terms of positions and titles. Then employees and managers feel limited. ("You've been doing a great job, but I can't promote you because there aren't any positions open" or "You're the best of the marketing assistants, but we've already got a director, so how about if we create a title for you, like senior marketing assistant in charge of words?")
> An effective coaching manager finds a way to move good employees forward without positions or titles.

soldiers could receive rapid advancement (field promotions) as reward for their deeds under fire. Your ability to confer stripes and stars on those in your own platoon is more limited, of course, but the ability to climb the ladder through excellent performance is a powerful inducement for some employees.

> ## Don't Make a Promotion the Payoff
> Can a promotion be a mistake? If a person works hard and earns it, it's only fair, right?
> Not necessarily. A promotion can be a very expensive mistake, in two ways.
> If employees get the feeling that a promotion is just a payoff for "putting in time" and not recognition of their ability to handle more responsibility, they're likely to do less. So, when you promote an employee, be sure that the promotion is not only a reward, showing thanks, but also a challenge, bestowing new responsibilities.
> The second way in which a promotion can be a mistake is related to the Peter Principle. In this case, a person is promoted to a position beyond his or her competence. We all know of instances in which this has happened.

Money and rank may be the biggest and most obvious tangible rewards, but they're not the only ones. Other effective rewards include time off (comp time, extra vacation; from a few hours to a sabbatical) and perks (the proverbial "key to the executive washroom," a reserved parking space, more flexible hours, an office with a window, and box seats at the local sports venue, just to mention a few).

When choosing among tangible rewards as motivational tools for your employees, be sure to bring in your coaching skills. *Ask* them what

---

GET CREATIVE!

SMART

Tangible rewards don't have to be money. Sometimes a small reward—like a gift card to a coffee shop, tickets to a sporting event, or even a charitable donation—can be surprisingly motivating to employees and teams. You know your staff best, so **MANAGING** think about what kind of rewards they like, both individually and as a group. Smaller rewards for successful projects or outcomes go a long way toward creating a positive work environment. Be creative in how you choose and offer rewards.

---

they want or what would motivate them! Listen to them consistently, and you'll be able to choose the right reward for the right person or team. Never make assumptions about what someone wants.

Symbolic Rewards

This is the category of trophies, trinkets, and toys—tangible items that have little or no monetary value but are invested with symbolic significance (if the giver and the recipient both believe in that value). Such rewards might include "Worker of the Week/Month/Year" trophies and plaques, leadership or sales awards, a profile in the in-house newsletter, a picture in the hallway Heroes Gallery, and a mouse pad with the company logo. Some of the best symbolic awards are traditional, such as a recognition dinner at which employees gather to honor one or more from among them.

You might want to establish several levels of symbolic rewards. Confer the highest ones in a ceremony that connotes their importance, but keep those to a minimum.

TRINKET ALERT!

CAUTION

Symbolic rewards can easily lose their significance if they're overdone. Don't overuse them or they won't be valuable to the recipients. Don't oversell them or nobody will take them seriously. Don't endlessly offer company-branded promotional items (a mouse pad with the company logo doesn't mean much as a reward if it's also a giveaway offered on customer orders).

Bestow the lower levels of symbolic rewards with a mixture of goodwill and humor—perhaps with mock seriousness but not real solemnity. Everyone will laugh along with the recipient, while secretly hoping for a turn.

Intangible Rewards

Many people assume that money is the primary positive motivator for peak performance. But surveys of worker attitudes show money in only fourth or fifth place on the list of motivators. Intangibles like "job satisfaction," "chances to learn," and "independence" consistently take the top spots in the rankings.

Reward workers by trusting and empowering them. Give them greater control over their work lives and allow for increased responsibility—as long as you link it with the authority and resources needed fpr the new role.

Provide opportunities for workers to increase mastery and skill, learn and grow, take ownership of and pride in their work. They'll strive to achieve the rewards that are inherent in the performance itself, independent of your judgment of that performance.

Provide the means and the opportunities. They'll do the rest.

Your coaching skills are invaluable here. By connecting with each person on a level that helps him or her develop skills and capabilities, you've been providing the intangible rewards all along. By helping them grow in their roles and beyond, you provide the atmosphere for success that feeds into these difficult-to-quantify rewards.

Rules of Rewarding

There are three simple points to keep in mind when rewarding employees. Link the reward to the behavior, confer rewards fairly, and make sure all employees understand how the rewards are given.

Link the Reward to the Behavior

A reward will reinforce action only if it comes as a consequence of that action—and employees know it. You can call it a merit raise, but if it comes for some reason other than meritorious performance, it will either reinforce some other behavior (endurance leading to longevity, most likely) or fail to reinforce anything.

You can link performance and reward in several ways.

- The reward can be given when a worker meets or exceeds established performance standards. For example, "Meet your sales goal and you get a performance bonus."

- Special merit awards can recognize performance above existing standards in quantity and/or quality.
- Rewards can derive from completion of the task itself.

Be sure that when explaining how the rewards are given, you clearly link them to specific outcomes. If you give a bonus to "top sellers," you'll need to clarify what you mean. This might be the top five salespeople (by total dollars of sales), the top three salespeople by total volume of units, top six for repeat sales or new customers, and so on. The requirements are clearly outlined, and a person will have a definite goal (SMART goal) to work toward. An employee will know whether he or she has qualified for the reward, and you might instill an atmosphere of friendly competition among your team.

GET EVEN MORE SPECIFIC SMART

MANAGING
In addition to being clear about the outcomes and criteria you are seeking, be sure to be explicit about what the reward is. Promising "a raise," "a bonus," "a special gift" is nice, but still unclear. To motivate employees to achieve, describe in detail what the reward is, so they can begin to visualize something specific. Thus, you might offer a 7 percent raise, an extra 5 percent commission bonus, four days of paid vacation, a three-day trip to Las Vegas, or a free dinner at a local upscale restaurant.

Confer the Reward Fairly

There's no place here for paying off friends or favoring pets. Although you'll never totally escape the subjective element in evaluating performance, you must base merit awards on objective, measurable standards as much as possible. For instance, production is relatively easy to measure objectively: At the end of the day (or week or month), you count the number of units manufactured, sold, painted, or installed. Strive to objectify your standards as much as possible, and, as discussed already, offer clear definitions of what "better performance" or "better behavior" means in context.

THE UNCOUNTABLE SMART
MANAGING
"Not everything that counts can be counted."
Although it's important to measure what workers do, we should never slip into neglecting the importance of things that are difficult or even impossible to measure, such as team spirit or dedication "above and beyond the call of duty."

EQUAL OPPORTUNITY

Equal access to the competition is not the same thing at all as equal access to the reward. "Fair" doesn't mean that over time the rewards will even out and everybody will get an equal share. All workers must have an equal opportunity to *compete* for the reward, but the rewards must go to those who *earn* them. Otherwise, you undermine the merit system.

Make sure everyone has equal opportunity to compete for the reward. Create specific performance goals, guidelines, and standards, and communicate them to all employees. Make sure all workers have the information, the equipment, and the materials they need to do the job.

Make Sure Employees Understand about the Rewards

Telling the truth and being believed are two different things. We've all known credible liars and sincere folks whom nobody quite trusts.

Being fair in your allocation of rewards and being seen as fair are, alas, two different things. You must be fair, and you must be sure everybody knows it.

Communicate and explain performance standards clearly. Announce merit awards publicly. Avoid the appearance (as well as the reality) of favoritism. Encourage all eligible workers to go for the rewards, not just your favorites or those you think have a good chance of earning them.

DON'T "TILT" THE SYSTEM

Reward carefully, to avoid the "tilt," the old tendency that "the rich get richer and poor get poorer."

Sometimes you may unintentionally encourage that sort of tilt. For example, if you reward your sales rep of the year with a Lexus, she may gain an advantage that will help her be on top the next year. Or if you reward your best administrative assistant with a faster computer and his own copy machine (those should be tools, not rewards!), he's likely to be even more efficient and have an edge over the other assistants.

These are just two fictitious examples. Look around you: Sometimes the truth is stranger than fiction. A word to the wise: Avoid encouraging the tilt.

The Coach as a Cheerleader

Your job as manager might be compared to that of a coach of an athletic team. A coach's activities—conducting practices, instructing, making out the starting line-up, planning strategy, calling plays, arguing with officials on behalf of the players—have their counterparts in your daily activities—training, assigning work, solving problems, giving feedback, negotiating with your bosses to get your staff what they need to do the job.

Most good managers perform one more important function: They root, root, root for the home team—loudly, passionately, and publicly. Managers may be their players' most vocal critics, but they're also their biggest cheerleaders. The coach approach of focusing on the positive and creating solutions also offers a way to cheer your team on and celebrate wins both big and small.

That's you, coach—the best cheerleader your players will ever have. Share their triumphs and their concerns. Exhort them to greater performance. Reward them with praise. Savor and celebrate their achievements without taking credit away from them.

Many of your employees won't think to thank you for being a great manager and coach. Some won't be aware of

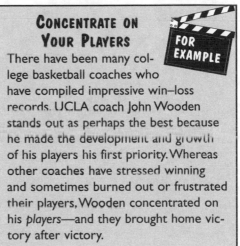

CONCENTRATE ON YOUR PLAYERS

FOR EXAMPLE

There have been many college basketball coaches who have compiled impressive win–loss records. UCLA coach John Wooden stands out as perhaps the best because he made the development and growth of his players his first priority. Whereas other coaches have stressed winning and sometimes burned out or frustrated their players, Wooden concentrated on his *players*—and they brought home victory after victory.

the extent to which you make their jobs more satisfying and their efforts more productive. But they will reward you with peak performance (and that's what you wanted all along).

The Coach's Checklist for Chapter 14

☑ Reward the performance you want.

☑ Tangible rewards provide valuable feedback only if employees connect them to individual performance.

☑ Rules of rewards: (1) link the reward to behavior, (2) confer the reward fairly, and (3) make sure all employees understand about the rewards.

☑ Be a cheerleader for your team. That's another intangible reward.

Chapter
15

Principles of Good Coaching (and Good Living)

H ere's your reward for reading this book: power principles that will raise you from the ranks of the merely excellent to the brilliant, whether you're coaching, managing, or just living.

The Principle of Getting Started

It doesn't matter where you start. It only matters *that* you start. Take action!

Action sometimes must precede understanding and almost always comes before certainty.

Don't wait for a problem to develop and grow before you start applying the techniques we've explored here. Don't wait to be inspired. Don't wait for insight. Don't get paralyzed by collecting data and information. Don't wait, period. Start *anywhere*. Work your way toward inspiration and insight. Look ahead to the future to create powerful solutions.

On any given project, get involved with coaching right up front, helping your employees define the issue, develop the approach, and create the action plan. It's much better to start out strong, smart, and together than to try to untangle the problem later. The time you spend at the front

TRICKS OF THE TRADE

Baby Steps

The journey of a thousand miles begins with a single step. You've certainly heard this truism before. Throughout this book we've talked about creating an action plan and breaking it down into individual steps. Get started! Even a small step is a movement in the right direction.

end of the project will return to you twofold in the problems you don't have to solve and the explanations you don't have to make later.

The Illusion of Control

You can't control anybody. You might be able to motivate them (if you know them well). You can direct their energies. You can teach them, lead them, praise them, and guide them.

But you can't *control* them—and you wouldn't want to if you could. You don't want compliant slaves. You want effective, independent workers. Throughout this book we've reminded you to focus on what you *can* control, and that does not include other people.

When you evaluate workers' performance and related workplace behaviors, put your perceptions to this test: "Is what they're doing *wrong*, or is it just *different*?" Remember that "different" doesn't necessarily equal "worse" or "bad." Let go of your judgments. You'll waste a lot of time and energy and engender a lot of anger and resentment making people undo and redo things they did fine but differently than how you would have.

Too many supervisors manage by the "my way or the highway" standard. They generally view differences as a threat to their authority.

Part of your job as a coach is to learn your employees' individual work styles and allow as much as possible for people to do it their way—as long as you get the result you want, when you want it.

The Principle of Decisions

"Not to decide is to decide," theologian Harvey Cox said.

If you fail to make a decision, or hem and haw until it's decided for you, you decide by default. You also abandon your role as leader and turn the fate of your project over to the prevailing winds.

Deciding not to act may be a valid choice. But failing to decide never is. Get as much information as you can, but remember to make the decision promptly. Cast your net wide for possible courses of action. Weigh carefully but quickly. Then decide. That's your responsibility as a manager.

Haste makes waste? Sometimes. But waiting makes nothing. Waste is a natural result of productivity. Throw away the waste, and you're left with a solution.

TIMELY DECISIONS   **SMART**

"The percentage of mistakes in quick decisions is no greater than in long-drawn-out vacillations," notes Anne O'Hare McCormick, "and the effect of decisiveness itself makes things go and creates confidence."

MANAGING

The Principle of Change

Change is inevitable and inexorable. When positive, it leads to growth, transformation, and whole new worlds of opportunities. When embraced, change can be a good thing. The whole idea of coaching is to create positive, sustainable change. People, groups, companies, industries, and the whole world change.

THOUGHTS, FEELINGS, ACTIONS

Many coaches work from the essential concept that thoughts lead to feelings, feelings lead to actions, and actions lead to results. If you want new actions (and new results), focusing on shifting the core thoughts will result in a lasting, natural change.   **TOOLS**

For instance, Joe believes that he's not a good public speaker (he has accepted this as part of his identity). This makes him feel anxious when asked to give a presentation, and his actions are avoiding it or trying to hand it off to someone else. (It also gives him an excuse not to improve, as he believes he is "just that way.") Through coaching, he decides to reverse this thought and starts to think "I am an effective presenter!" He starts to feel more confident just by thinking this new thought, and when asked to give a presentation, he agrees and gets to work. His actions flow from this new thought as if it was already true!

Change may be good and it's certainly inevitable, but that doesn't mean you have to change for change's sake. Change *wisely*. Refusing to change at all will leave you behind, but constantly changing just because something is new makes you lose any consistency and momentum you had going. A wise business manager evaluates and learns from the new buzzwords, trends, tools, markets, techniques, and movements before getting on the bandwagon. A good manager gets buy-in from his or her team, as well as support from executives, when instituting a major change.

The Principle of Time

Don't waste time—yours or theirs. Sure, that's easier said than done. Time is a resource everyone needs to get their tasks done. And it's a limited resource at that. Respect others' time and your own. You can make a big difference in the workplace by avoiding certain pervasive time eaters.

Memo Mania

Are you sure you have to write it down or type it out? If you really have to—no doubt so somebody can file it—be concise and clear. Don't assume your employees have read it just because you sent it to them.

Online communications have made it fast and convenient to fire off a note to all employees at once, but if you're sending out 50 messages a day, or marking them all "FYI," you've deluged your workers and wasted their time. You've also positioned yourself as someone who talks a lot but doesn't have much to say. Important messages will get lost in the shuffle.

Make sure the message is worth the ink and paper or electrons in the e-mail, then follow up to make sure employees got it and understand it.

Info Glut

Computers have made it possible to access virtually any information source in the world, if you can find it (and it's easier and easier to find it). We're all drowning in information, learning to put off decisions while we gather ever more data.

- Don't mistake information for knowledge.
- Don't mistake knowledge for wisdom.
- Don't mistake wisdom for an informed decision that gets the project moving.

Just because you can *get* the information doesn't mean you *have* to get it. Apply commonsense, reasonable guidelines, and set a time limit for your research.

If passing information on to your employees, don't overload them. They may need some information, but empower them to find out on their own, or provide what they need with resources for more learning. There's no need to send 10 pages of background info when all a person needs is one or two statistics.

Meeting Menace

People don't hate meetings. They hate nonsense. They hate wasting their time. They hate listening to someone read a list of announcements to them, when they could have selectively read (and skipped) them much faster themselves. And they really loathe spending a precious hour discussing an issue that matters to them, only to find out that a decision has already been made.

Hold meetings only for necessary interactions that can't take place any other way. Don't call for a meeting when a memo will be sufficient. Plan every meeting by setting an agenda. Circulate discussion items and needed information ahead of time. And run meetings tightly to respect time and tasks.

MEETING AGENDA **SMART**
Always go into a meeting with an agenda of some sort. You and everyone else involved should know what is up for **MANAGING** discussion (and what *isn't*). An agenda allows you to limit tangential conversations and irrelevant discussion. You show respect for everyone's time when you create and stick to an agenda.

Multiple Management

To the extent that you have the power to make it happen, make sure workers report to one and only one supervisor for any given project. Having to report to two bosses is a sure time waster. Define lines of responsibility and authority clearly and publicly. Don't pass the management buck, and don't let anybody else pass it, either.

Marilyn Monroe Complex

Don't make people wait. It's bad manners, and it's inefficient and ineffective managing.

Don't make appointments you can't keep. Don't show up late for a meeting, especially if you're running it. Don't make anybody wait on the phone while you take another call.

Making people wait wastes their time—and insults them. It conveys the clear message that you consider what you're doing to be a lot more important than interacting with them.

If you can't help being late, make sure you apologize to the group, quickly and sincerely. If you must explain, keep it short.

Trivial Pursuit

Effective time managers learn to ask themselves the Lakein Question (named for Alan Lakein, the progenitor of modern time management techniques): "Do I want or need to be doing this right now?"

Ask this question on behalf of employees, too. Don't give them something to do just so that they have something to do. That's how adults treat children—and it's a quick way to send a strong message about how you really view your employees. Find meaningful tasks that build to something. Remember to connect their tasks to larger goals—for them individually, for the department, the company. Empower your workers to get proactive in finding tasks so they aren't constantly coming to you for the next assignment.

Yes, the word *business* means the state of being busy. But there's no profit in simply keeping busy. Take the time to create meaningful work plans, as you coach employees toward being independent self-starters who solve problems without you.

The Principle of Questions

Ask *lots* of questions. As we mentioned early on in this book, asking questions taps into your employees' knowledge, shows them that you value their opinion, and helps bring forth many options for change and growth. Asking questions that probe for deeper meaning and creative responses is absolutely essential for good coaching.

What's the worst thing that could happen if you ask a dumb question? You'll reveal your ignorance, which may be

SMART   **ASK TO FIND OUT**
The best way to avoid mistakes is to ask questions. As Malcolm Forbes once
MANAGING observed, "One who never asks either knows everything or knows nothing." He also noted that "the smart ones ask when they don't know—and sometimes when they do."

a little embarrassing—an occasional price to pay for not being perfect. However, by asking you show your willingness to learn. What's the worst thing that could happen if you fail to ask questions? You *remain* ignorant.

The answers to a lot of questions may seem obvious, but they often help us gain insight and initiate creative breakthroughs.

The Principle of Mistakes

Everyone makes mistakes. Failures are inevitable. Admit them. Learn from them. Grow, and move on.

The folks who work with you know you're human. They'll have a lot more confidence in you when you show them that you know it, too.

If the notion of making a mistake bothers you, call it something else. Call it a learning opportunity.

The story of Thomas Edison and the light bulb is worth retelling in this context. Edison tried hundreds of materials, trying to find a filament that would heat up when an electric current passed through it, giving off light without burning up. After seemingly endless disappointments, there was still no guarantee that the idea would work at all.

When asked how he was able to endure so many mistakes, Edison reportedly said that he hadn't considered any of his attempts to be failures. He was simply learning what wouldn't work.

Mistakes teach us what doesn't work. That's valuable information. From that, we can start to figure out what *does* work. Failure gives us the opportunity to learn and grow. We become larger than the failure.

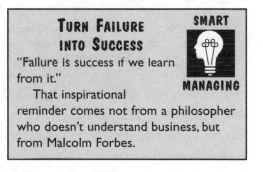

TURN FAILURE INTO SUCCESS

SMART MANAGING

"Failure is success if we learn from it."

That inspirational reminder comes not from a philosopher who doesn't understand business, but from Malcolm Forbes.

When you fall short of your goal, learn and go on. Redefine your goal, alter your approach, and get help. You only truly fail when you don't get back up after being knocked down.

The Principle of Anger

When it comes to anger, follow this guideline: Feel it, but don't act on it. A worker screws up and you lash out, administering a vicious public reprimand. It's only natural. You're righteously mad. All your hard work is wasted in a stupid, careless second. The worker had it coming. Besides, if you try to bottle up all that anger, you're courting a heart attack or a stroke. Let it all out. Vent that spleen. It's better for you, right?

Feeling anger—along with frustration and disappointment—is natural. But you don't have to *let* the feeling dictate or control your actions. Ride out the adrenaline rush with a few deep breaths and some calm self-talk. Feel the anger, acknowledge that it's valid, and then release it. If you can't handle the situation yet, walk away until you can. Then do the right thing, instead of the natural thing.

KNOW THYSELF

TOOLS
Smart people can handle their anger well when they have a deep knowledge of themselves. It starts with knowing what kinds of things make you angry, so that you can be aware of when those kinds of things are coming your way (if possible) and prepare yourself emotionally. If you know how you best like to process anger, employ those techniques when angry. For instance, you might need to vent to a noninvolved person, take a long walk or drive to calm down, or have a brief screaming fit and throw a few things. If you know how you best release anger, you can be ready to move forward. Also, remember to respect how your employees deal with anger, too, as it may be different from how you handle it.

"Anger, if not restrained, is frequently more harmful than the wrong that provoked it." That sentence is as true now as it was when Seneca spoke it about 2,000 years ago. You can't undo a mistake or change the past. But if you act in anger, you're probably going to make the situation worse.

If you hold on to your anger, you'll fester in resentment and stop trusting your team members. Your negative emotion will drag your employees down into that anger pit with you, and then things will get really bad.

It's natural to feel anger (it's a valid emotion), and you shouldn't bottle it up. But do know how to vent it appropriately and release it, so you can move on into positive action.

The Illusion of Objectivity

There is no such thing as pure objectivity. Managers are supposed to be objective, to view the situation without emotion, to judge dispassionately, to rule infallibly. Professional coaches work hard to maintain as objective a viewpoint as possible (knowing that pure objectivity isn't entirely possible) to help their clients reach clarity.

The reality is, you don't check your humanity at the door when you show up for work in the morning. You bring all of you to the task—your knowledge and experience, your empathy and understanding, your ambition and disappointment, your opinions and prejudices. So do your employees.

You're going to like some workers more than others. You'll find some a lot easier to talk with. You'll appreciate those who seem most cooperative, most in tune with your philosophy and your ways of doing things, while resenting those who seem to fight you every step of the way. It's only natural.

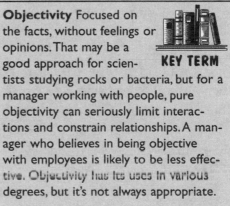

Objectivity Focused on the facts, without feelings or opinions. That may be a good approach for scientists studying rocks or bacteria, but for a manager working with people, pure objectivity can seriously limit interactions and constrain relationships. A manager who believes in being objective with employees is likely to be less effective. Objectivity has its uses in various degrees, but it's not always appropriate.

KEY TERM

In short, you'll respond to people as a person. And that means you'll be *subjective*.

Don't hide your biases from yourself. Own up to them and then compensate for these "natural" feelings to be sure you're being fair to all employees—whether you particularly like them or not.

The Principle of the Big Picture

Don't sweat the small stuff. Conventional wisdom has this one half right. You don't have enough physical, emotional, and psychic energy to squander on the dozens of daily (and sometimes inconsequential) crises that nip at you in the workplace. Keep your perspective, your priorities, and your balance. Your job is to think bigger anyway and provide that bridge between workers on the line and the upper management and goals of the whole organization. The small stuff can serve you, and be indicative of larger things going on below the surface. Remember to look deeper and make connections.

Your decisions really do matter—for your organization, the people who work with you, and your own sense of integrity and worth. You'll face lots of big challenges that deserve all the sweat, all the concern and thought and effort you can give them. Make sure you've got enough resources in reserve when these challenges come.

The Principle of Fear

A Chinese proverb advises you to stop running and face the monster that is chasing you. When you do, you often find that the monster isn't so scary after all.

Fear needn't cripple you. Courage is, after all, acting in the face of your fear, not in the absence of fear. Trying to avoid the confrontation that frightens you only makes you incapable of right action. If you don't face your fears, you allow them greater power over you.

Fear itself can't hurt you. In fact, when you're able to focus it, fear can keep you alert and give you energy. It's a tool, a signal for you to be alert and wary. It's not a stop sign.

Feel your fear. Then do the right thing anyway.

The Principle of Role Modeling

The workplace needs clear lines of authority, well-defined responsibility, and accountability for actions done and not done.

You want respect from your workers. Respect them. You want them to listen to you. Listen to them. You want them to withhold criticism when brainstorming for solutions to problems. Then stifle yours.

You can talk the talk, but to be truly effective, you must walk the walk. Treat others exactly as you would have them treat you. That rule truly is golden, and it's the smartest advice on human relations you can ever give or get.

The Principle of Life

You are not your job. Your ultimate worth is not in your work or your paycheck. You don't have to earn the right to exist. Who you are isn't limited or defined by what you do. In fact, the reverse is true: What you do flows from who you are.

Devote time and energy to your life outside of work. Create a balance that respects all the aspects of your personhood and gives you a full life. It will make you a better worker. You can develop a profound sense of satisfaction, contentment, and joy.

Nobody ever said, "I wish I'd spent more time at the office."

What if you died tomorrow? What would you most regret never having done? (We bet it's not something from your work to-do list.)

Now you know the core skills and techniques to be an effective coach in the workplace. For that matter, you might have already known a lot of it when you started reading this book. You may have never seen it all put down in one place before, and you may have needed to have your own good instincts confirmed in print.

Coaching isn't only about knowing. It's about doing. *Coach* stops being a noun, a name for your relationship with your workers, and becomes a verb, the way you interact with your team every day.

The Coach's Checklist for Chapter 15

☑ Review the principles and concepts in this chapter. They will work for you on the job and in your life off the job as well.

Index